BAYOU
UNDERGROUND

BAYOU
UNDERGROUND

Tracing the Mythical Roots
of American Popular Music

DAVE THOMPSON

ECW Press

Published by ECW Press, 2120 Queen Street East, Suite 200,
Toronto, Ontario, Canada M4E 1E2
416.694.3348 / info@ecwpress.com

LIBRARY AND ARCHIVES CANADA CATALOGUING IN PUBLICATION

Thompson, Dave, 1960 Jan. 3-
Bayou underground / Dave Thompson.

ISBN 978-1-55022-962-2

1. Music—Gulf Coast (U.S.)—History. 2. Popular music—United
States—History.

I. Title.

ML200.T469 2010   780.976   C2010-901374-3

Editor: Jen Hale
Text design: Tania Craan
Cover design: David Gee
Cover images: © AVTG (swamp); © Sandra O'Claire (piano)
All photos and illustrations are from the author's private collection
Typesetting: Mary Bowness
Printing: Thomson-Shore 1 2 3 4 5

This book is printed on paper that is 30% recycled / post-consumer waste product.

FSC
www.fsc.org
MIX
Paper from
responsible sources
FSC® C013483

PRINTED AND BOUND IN THE UNITED STATES

ECW PRESS
ecwpress.com

Louisiana . . . exudes a simultaneously attractive and repulsive exoticism, not least for outsiders too lazy to learn the difference between Cajun and Creole or how to pronounce New Orleans correctly. An exoticism definitely exists, but not in the muddled, commercial, and mythical vision of corruption, drugs, Voodoo, poly-sexuality, bourbon, gambling, degeneracy, and disguise; wherein addled quasi-Klansmen and octoroons, knee-deep in headless chickens and armed to the teeth, ride through swamps and housing projects on giant crawfish, speaking in tongues, blasting trumpets, leaping off French Quarter balconies, eating their young and selling their souls. All while covered in powdered sugar.

D. M. Edwards, Popmatters.com

TABLE OF CONTENTS

INTRODUCTION

A stranger stopped in front of an old house to ask directions. The decrepit octogenarian on the tumbledown porch replied, "Well, you carry on down this road until you come to . . . ," and he named a local landmark, lost in a fire in 1953. "You turn left, and cross the field until you reach . . . ," and he named another landmark, washed away in the flood of 1927. "And then you just keep on going until you get to . . ." and he named a third, one that even local lore could only place in an approximate vicinity. "And it'll be right across from there."

"Hell," said the stranger. "If I knew where all those places were, I wouldn't be needing directions."

And the old fellow replied, "Well, if you need directions, maybe you don't have any business going there."

— Louisiana fable

It's not true that the people around here are unfriendly, that they don't take kindly to strangers, that they are silent and secretive, especially with outsiders. But it is true that they like to keep themselves to themselves, and if a visitor finds himself on the wrong end of a local joke . . . "well, maybe if you don't know it's a joke, you have no business listening to what the people are saying in the first place."

I've been hearing those words, and appreciating that sentiment, for more than two decades. It was 1986 when I first visited Louisiana, a getaway that lasted a weekend or so, but which was destined to be repeated over and over. Even then, though, it wasn't chance that brought me here. Rather, it was a fascination that occasionally bordered on obsession, a need to understand how America could have nurtured such a non-American place, and how that very non-American-ness had itself created a culture of its own, redolent of so many other places, but unique as well, a singular slice of life that was French and Spanish and Caribbean in one breath, and none of those things in the other.

I walked, I talked, I traveled around, and with every step a fresh thought hit me: a line from a song, a phrase from a book, a snatch of melody or a flicker of movie footage. And I wondered, what would happen if you took all of these things and blended them together into one single story?

Something, I hope, like this.

Two books set this one in motion. The first, which I wish I'd had time to reread while I was writing, was Anne Rice's *Interview with the Vampire* — groundbreaking when it was originally published in 1976, but subsequently so overwrought in the annals of popular literature that maybe it's just as well that I never dug it out again. But, if any book can be said to have canonized a certain image of Louisiana in general, and New Orleans in particular, into the popular mythos, at least in the years before Sookie Stackhouse came fang-banging into view, it was this one.

The second was Barry Jean Ancelet's *Cajun and Creole Folktales*, which is exactly what it says on the cover. Its veracity was brought home to me when I found more or less the same tale that opens this introduction reiterated within its pages. Ancelet considers it a cultural in-joke, by the way, but that doesn't detract from its accuracy.

His book reminds us of one of the most crucial truths there is: that folklore and legend might not document history *as it is remembered*. They remember it as it was, from the perspective of the people who actually lived through it, and, before you write that off as merely a fanciful whim, think back to the stirring times that you have lived through, and remember what affected you most. The big picture that will be recalled in the histories of the future, or the minutiae that you experienced firsthand? Because every time you retell your anecdote, and somebody else retells it to his or her friends, you are creating a folklore of your own. You just don't, as did the folk of ages past, make a literal song and dance of it.

Equally crucial was Mike Tidwell's *Bayou Farewell*, with its masterful re-creation of a way of life that the tour books don't like to talk about; and a fourth influence presented itself completely out of left field, in the form of Lady Alice McCloud's latter-day classic of BDSM-flavored erotica, *Whalebone Strict*, which reimagines modern-day Louisiana from behind the gauze of a fantastical steam punk splendor. Add to this a fifth volume that arrived while I was writing, Judith Kelleher Schafer's *Brothels, Depravity and Abandoned Women: Illegal Sex in Antebellum New Orleans*, and my on-the-road library was complete.

All five volumes paint a very different portrait of the region; all five sit very uneasily on the shelf together, conjoined by geography but otherwise boasting absolutely nothing in common with one another. But it's that very diversity that binds them — five different approaches to an identical state of mind. There is something in the air down here, in the water and in the land, something that plaits its people to it more completely than any place else in the United States; there's a sense that the people *are* the land, and that one without the other is just so much blood or mud, shifting aimlessly in search of something to give it substance.

As a complete outsider, traveler and tourist, I first found that substance in music, years before I had even imagined journeying to the source of the sounds themselves. But once I did, once I got here, I knew that there was a lot more to my quest than simply a wild night in the French Quarter. Louisiana is home to some of the most unique music in America, the collision of a multitude of cultures and communities, of indigenous instinct and imported impressions, an unparalleled world whose arms reach out not only from New Orleans, but also from every corner of the state. Music is everywhere, blasting from the clubs on Bourbon Street of course, but also strumming from porches and keening beside campfires, a soundscape that doesn't simply soundtrack life, it helps dictate it.

Babies are sung into the world, and, at the end of life, they are serenaded out again. Of all the scenes in James Bond's *Live and Let Die* that establish the mood and nature of that movie, it is the powerful New Orleans funeral that opens the action: swaying mourners, swinging musicians and respectful onlookers. Pause now to ask yourself, is there any other city in the world whose flavor could be conveyed by a few minutes spent watching a funeral cortege? Elsewhere in America, death is terrifying, shut away and cloaked in generic religious scripture and parable. Here, it is a celebration, sending off the lost loved one in the most beautiful and moving way imaginable.

The explosion of interest in world music that swept out of a few fringe cults in the 1990s and saw, for a time, every record store in the land reconfigure their stock according to an artist's country of origin brought an especial boom to Louisiana, for better and — of course, because where human nature leads, major commercial interests will surely follow — for worse.

Dedicated followers of genuine musical authenticity lost little time in mourning the speed with which an entire wave of nouveau culture vultures descended upon the region to bestow their blessings, and their own interpretations, upon musical forms that had remained unchanged for decades. New devotees did not even consider that their attentions would irrevocably alter and ultimately distort the very heritage they were seeking to secure.

Purity can exist only in a vacuum of its own creation. Outside forces do permeate that bubble, but they do so because they are invited in and absorbed organically. Thrust them in without any understanding of what they are being thrust into, and the situation shifts dramatically and, usually, irreversibly.

Cajun music has barely changed in the years since it was first packaged up on a Putumayo CD. But it is not the same as it used to be either. In New Orleans, a city that once had nothing to do with the sounds of its surroundings, because it had created so many of its own already, was inundated by earnest young fiddlers with a knapsack full of songs, and most of them probably came from New Jersey. You know them. They're the ones whom you talk to after a night of beautiful music, and when you ask them what one of the songs was about, they reply, "I don't know. It's in French. But the vocal sounds are amazing, aren't they?" A new musical genre was born, and a generation has now grown up listening to it. It's called "parrot folk."

"It wasn't that long ago," sighed songwriter Jerry Reed, "that if you wanted to hear authentic Cajun music, you had to go to authentic Cajun country and hunt those old men down. Today you can simply head on down to Barnes & Noble, and it's all there waiting for you. It's a lot easier like that, but you know? It's not so much fun anymore."

Today, zydeco and Cajun music regularly appear on the world music charts; the acclaimed compilations of both the Putumayo and Rough Guide series feature the music heavily in their catalogs. The sound has spread across the world, too. From Belgium, the Big Bayou Bandits captivate modern listeners with their steaming brand of Cajun music; from Canada, the Bayou Boys offer a gripping tribute to Creedence Clearwater Revival's most exhilarating past. Today, more people than ever know the names, sing the songs and recite the legends of the region.

But that is all they can do. They do not feel the damp, smell the swamp and startle when they hear the rustling behind them. The mystique of the bayou is still there, of course, for how could anything so primeval be chased out by the limelight? But the lights can blind us regardless.

"The minute you land in New Orleans," writer Tom Robbins once said, "something wet and dark leaps on you and starts humping you like a swamp dog in heat." New Orleans is not, and has never been, wholly impervious to the sounds of its environs. It's just that it is always easier to ignore the tumult on your doorstep if that of elsewhere is coming in louder. Just as a citizen of one city barely even notices the local attractions that make the tourists gawp (how many Seattle-ites, for example, spend their days excitedly watching and filming the doings at the fish market?), so a would-be jazzman in 1920s New Orleans would have had no interest at all in the folk sounds down the road.

But they crept in anyway, in that subtle way that, again, is universal. No matter whether or not artists are aware of their presence, cultural reference points will almost always sneak into their work in some way. Whether it's an English author dropping into his latest novel references to some dimly remembered childhood confectionary, or an American rock band that cannot help but remind you of vintage KISS, you can take the kid away from his roots, but you can't get the roots out of the kid.

First, though, we have to get there.

Step off your flight and into the arrivals terminal at Louis Armstrong New Orleans International Airport, and you can sense it immediately, a taste in your mouth, a smell in your nose and a punch in your stomach. Other cities exist in tight little bubbles, constructed entirely from their own concrete and glass. But not New Orleans. For almost 300 years now, the city has lived, breathed and eaten the land from which it was carved and upon which it was built. Even at the city's height, it was hard to escape the feeling that it was only man's determination that kept that land at bay — or, at least, the waters. Building any kind of settlement around 10 feet below sea level requires an awful lot of faith in man's technological genius. Building a major city there demanded faith in the power of miracles as well. It still does. But, as the havoc wrought by Hurricane Katrina is finally (but so slowly) pushed back into memory, and the city dwellers continue rebuilding their shattered lives, New Orleans remains what it always was, the heart and soul of American popular music, the birthplace of some of its most enduring styles, songs and performers, and the cradle in which jazz, R & B, rock 'n' roll and so much more were each carefully nurtured.

Step outside of the city, and the mood shifts violently. The passage of time has altered the country irrevocably. Even before Katrina came to chew up landscapes and landmarks alike, and Deepwater Horizon drenched nature's own recovery in oil, industry, navigation and simple civilization had torn apart some of America's most evocative territory — that endless maze of forest and swamp that the locals called the bayou, from the Choctaw Indian word *bayuk*, meaning "slow stream." Indeed, the word *bayou* still refers to a single piece of slow-moving water. But the bayou has taken on a meaning of its own regardless, and is a world of its own — a misty, marshy, sometimes treacherous, oft-times sinister land of creeping darkness and living shadows, secret legends and livid mythology. And music. A lot of music.

It is that darkness and those shadows that permeate *Bayou Underground*. About 15 years ago, sitting in a bar in Thibodaux, Louisiana, an old Cajun guitar player told me that only a fool would try to pin the spirit of the bayou down in a book, and only an idiot would try to argue with the words. "There's no right or wrong. Either you feel it or you don't, but even if you do, what you feel is nothing like what I feel, and what I feel has nothing to do with what somebody else feels."

He was right, too, although it took me a while to figure that out — which is why this is not a book about Louisiana music, Cajun fiddlers or zydeco acolytes. It is about the music that makes you *think* of those things, but a whole lot more as well: a lighthearted and not altogether well-behaved exploration of what the bayou has come to mean . . . *not* to the locals who call this region home, but to the tourists who flock here every year, and to people who have never even set foot in a swamp, whose sole exposure to the sights and sounds of the area is drawn from the dents it has made in popular culture. Picture Bond braving voodoo magic in *Live and Let Die*; Eric

Burdon bemoaning a life in the House of the Rising Sun; Anne Rice kick-starting a whole new cultural mythology with *Interview with the Vampire*; Thrift Moncrieff being bound and buggered in a tumbledown swamp shack. Billy and Wyatt, the freewheelin' heroes of the movie *Easy Rider*, met their demise in Louisiana, on a stretch of Highway 105 between Krotz Springs and Melville. So did the legendary depression-era outlaws Bonnie Parker and Clyde Barrow, on Highway 154, outside Gibsland, Bienville Parish. I'll bet the moment you read that, chances are that either Georgie Fame or Serge Gainsbourg (or Roger McGuinn and the Holy Modal Rounders) started playing in your head. That's what this book is about, those moments when the mere mention of something can kick-start a soundtrack in your mind.

Delving deep into what some locals like to call "the northernmost tip of the Caribbean," and which others simply refer to as "south of the South," *Bayou Underground* is less a narrative and more a patchwork quilt, then: an assortment of stories and legends, observations and mythologies, histories and recipes, all bound together by the songs that best capture those moments when you know you're alone, in the darkness and green, but you know you're not alone either. Because there's something else out there, and maybe . . . just maybe . . . it's hungry. *Bayou Underground* flourishes in the daylight as well, to unearth the myriad skeins of history that have, over the past three centuries, either arisen from the swamplands themselves, or been drawn from fellow visitors to the region, as they seek to set down for posterity the emotions, dreams and enchantments that the area instilled in them.

Some are household names.

We meet Dr. John the Night Tripper, the psychedelic voodoo man who walked on gilded splinters and left gris-gris on your doorstep. Voodoo is alive in the bayou (or so the guidebooks will tell you), and when Dr. John — plain old Malcolm "Mac" John Rebennack Jr. to his family and friends — first took to the stage in the mid-1960s, it was alive there as well.

We visit the House of the Rising Sun, the most famous bordello in America long before the Animals took its name to the top of the charts in 1964.

We hunt 'gators with Amos Moses, the one-armed Cajun back-woodsman documented by country songwriter Jerry Reed, but immortalized in legend long before that. "Sure can get lost in the Louisiana bayou," sang Reed of the local sheriff, missing-presumed-dead after one stakeout too many. But he was not the first would-be law enforcer to be swallowed without trace by the marshland mists.

We don't even stay in Louisiana, although we always come back there in the end. We dance and dine with the young Elvis Presley in the early 1950s in Memphis, Tennessee. We have some hummingbird cake outside Natchez, Mississippi. We write a song on the road with the Alice Cooper Band, and wind down Highway 61 to find out if God and Abraham are still trading barbs there.

We'll also hear from tourists who came to the swamplands and were irreversibly altered by the experience. We hang with Bo Diddley (the author of "Who Do You Love," a pulse-pounding, soul-churning invocation of bayou mysticism at its most primal . . . "I walk 47 miles of barbed wire, use a cobra snake for a necktie") and share a figurative bowl of gumbo with Nick Cave, whose muse has regularly drawn deep from that same well of inspiration.

We walk with Bob Dylan and recall Creedence Clearwater Revival, who may have grown up in California, but whose boots were nevertheless caked with bayou mud. Their second album was even titled *Bayou Country*, and it seethes with imagery that could have been forged no place else.

We spend less time than I expected to with the unsung heroes of the bayou, the folk who lived and worked here their entire lives, and whose music — some of it captured by passing folklorists like Mina Monroe and Alan Lomax — told the true tale of bayou life. But we do sit down for a killer bowl of jambalaya with Hank Williams, and if you've ever wondered how to make alligator burgers, step right this way.

Oh, and one final point. The songs that introduce each chapter are the ones that accompanied me as I traveled the region, because they're the songs that reminded me where I was. Occasionally they may dovetail with the chapter itself, sometimes they're just a flash at the back of your eardrum, and sometimes they have nothing to do with what you're reading, so please don't turn to Chapter Five and expect to learn all about Joe Satriani. Because you won't. But if you put the songs on a mix-tape, and let your imagination trail in my footsteps, you'll understand why they're here. Part social history, part travelogue, and part lament for a way of life that has now all but disappeared, *Bayou Underground* is a cultural iPod stuffed with mythology and then purposely set to shuffle. It is the story of American music's forgotten adolescence, and the parentage it barely even knows about. By comparison, the Big Easy had it easy.

TRACK
ONE

"Promised Land" by Elvis Presley
from the LP *Promised Land* (RCA)
1975

"Swamp rock" is a horrible term, but every time I attempted to explain to friends what this book was about (friends, that is, who actually care enough about their music to try to slap intellectual labels on it) someone always stopped me halfway through my explanation, raised a hand and then pronounced knowledgeably, "Ah, you mean swamp rock."

Do I?

To me, swamp rock has always sounded like something that was bred by the Cramps in the sewers of late seventies New York City, nurtured by the Gun Club, obsessed on by the psychobilly movement and last seen heading towards Japan, where all the musical dinosaurs seem to flourish forever.

I suppose, if I was to pause for a moment, I *could* conceive of another definition — but after 30 years spent writing about rock and pop in all of their most fashionable guises, I'd had enough of labels for a while, and wanted to try my hand at something else . . . a musical style that wasn't simply indefinable in general terms, it probably only existed in my own imagination.

Even with the headphones on, and a homemade CD pumping mud through my bloodstream, I struggled to discern any coherent musical thread that united Alice Cooper screaming "Black Juju" and Nick Cave lionizing the killer "Stagger Lee," between the Sensational Alex Harvey Band celebrating "Amos Moses" and Creedence Clearwater Revival hearing something through the grapevine. Add a little Robert Johnson to the brew . . . but only because I couldn't find my tape of Wild Willy Barrett doing "Me and the Devil Blues," a jag of Juicy Lucy and a generous helping of Sinead O'Connor, and the picture became murkier by the moment.

Except it also became clearer, because the songs I was selecting had nothing to do with any musical style — real, invented or even imagined. They were a mindset, a state of being that existed some-where between a road map and a ghost story, between the lies that the tourist guides tell out-of-towners, and the truths that they won't even tell themselves. And, if you could then distil that mindset down to one single fragment of recognizable reality, it would probably look a lot like a swamp. Which rocks.

So, swamp rock?

Maybe so.

But not in the way that my well-meaning friends meant.

In 1983, rocker Johnnie Allan described swamp rock, its history, mystery and convoluted development, thus. "It's the musicians who make the sound different. Those guys, Jivin' Gene, T. K. Hulin — virtually all of them speak French and some of them played in French accordion bands just like I did. Consequently, I think we all kept part of this French-Cajun music ingrained in us; you can detect it, something of a Cajun flavor in the song."

For Allan, that flavor erupted out of what is still his best-known recording, an ingenious rewiring of Chuck Berry's "Promised Land," which sounds as fresh and exciting today as it did when he cut it in 1964. Born in Rayne, Louisiana, and a steel guitarist before he started rocking, Allan has been credited with being the first to mash the mutant new genre — for that's what rock 'n' roll was back then — with anything approaching a traditional form, and he did it with such an air of insouciance that it's easy to believe he didn't even think about it. He just took the music he loved and the music he loved to play and married them together across one of Chuck's most endearing three-chord travelogues, and every great version of the song to have come along since then owes something or other to Johnnie Allan's prototype.

All except for one of them.

In 1983, journalist Bill Miller traced the birth of swamp rock . . . or swamp-pop or Cajun rock or Bayou beat, as sundry other critics termed the sound, narrowing it down to the 400 miles of highway that stretch from Port Arthur, Texas, to New Orleans, and which are fringed almost every step of the way by the tiny towns and villages whose local music scene developed down such secret byways that, only when all the component parts were placed together, could anything even remotely resembling unity be discerned.

Miller wrote, "There are Lake Charles and Ville Platte, the home of Floyd Soileau's Jin and Swallow labels; Abbeville, where Bobby Charles lives in hermit-like seclusion; Crowley, where Jay Miller recorded the finest Excello blues, and such outposts of swampland as the aptly named Cut Off, Joe Barry's home."

So that's what Bill Miller said swamp rock was, and we have no reason at all to argue. He's right. In fact, if you want to dig even deeper, you can increase the banquet another hundredfold.

Early Elvis Presley and the Sun Records label clash with Joe Falcon, who made the first ever Cajun records back in the late 1920s. Fats Domino and Warren Storm. Earl King, whose "Those Lonely, Lonely Nights," said Dr. John, "is a classic South Louisiana two-chord — E-flat, B-flat — slow ballad." And, back in 1969, with the swamp rock term first coming into fashionable play in the pages of the music press, record producer Jerry Wexler explained it to *Billboard* in a way that left it even more up in the air than before:

*It is the Southern sound! R & B played by Southern whites!
It is up from Corpus Christi, Thibodaux, Florence, Tupelo,
Helena, Tuscaloosa, Memphis! It is the flowering of the new
Southern life style! It is Duane Allman [...] It is Southern
rhythm sections made up of young country cats that began
with Hawkshaw Hawkins and turned left behind Ray
Charles and [Bobby] "Blue" Bland. It is Joe South and his
great gift of melody, and the lowest-tuned guitar this side of
"Pop" Staples. It is the spirit of Willie Morris, born in the
Delta, schooled in Texas, and arrived on the literary scene
in New York as editor of* Harper's *at 32, and who, with
Faulkner, calls the black people of his home his kin.*

*It's country funk. The Byrds put something in it, Ray
Charles added a lot. It's a pound of R & B, and an ounce
or three of country. The music has Cajun swamp miasma,
a touch of Longhair's New Orleans blues rumba, some of
Taj's recreations or Cow Cow Davenport's buck dance
thing. It has been shaped by Otis Redding's horn thinking,
Steve Cropper's and Reggie Young's and Chips Moman's
fantastic section guitar work – part lead and part rhythm
on the same tune.*

*It has Tommy Cogbill's structured variations of the rhap-
sodic Motown bass lines. It has Roger Hawkins' gut-stirring,
beautiful snare hit. Jim Stewart and Rick Hall and Chips
and Tom Dowd picked up where Sam Phillips left off and
poured it into Sam & Dave and Clarence Carter. It's a lot
of gospel changes and very, very rarely 12-bar blues. It's not
rockabilly, either, but the echoes of early Sun are there.
Ghosts of beginning Elvis and Cash and Vincent. Listen to
'Suspicious Minds' live, with the Sweets backing Elvis, and
that's definitely it.*

And listen to Elvis' "Promised Land," recorded in December 1973 at the Stax Studios in Memphis, and that's definitely "it" as well. Indeed, listen to anything Elvis sang in the mid-1950s, when he was still young and hungry, the late 1960s, when he was bored with everything else, and the early 1970s, when he really did wake up for a while, and it's irrelevant what the material's like, he imbues it with that same breath regardless. So it doesn't matter how much I wanted to talk about Tony Joe White, the Oak Grove Swamp Fox, the subject kept coming back round to Elvis.

Not that there's anything wrong with that. Half the civilized world would never have heard of Tony Joe if it wasn't for Elvis recording his "Polk Salad Annie," and we might never have heard of Elvis either, if it wasn't for the *Louisiana Hayride*, and who cares if you needed to hitch all the way up to Shreveport to see him perform there.

A televised festival of country, pop and proto-rock, the first *Hayride* was staged in 1948, the last in 1960, but in between times it kicked out a wave of talent that the *Opry* and the *Ozark Jubilee* could only dream of. For while they all showcased established stars, the *Hayride* made room for the up'n'comers as well — Elvis was still an unknown teenager the first time he appeared, in 1954, pushing his debut single to a markedly lukewarm response. But just a year later he was back, and things were a little different by then.

Tony Joe never played the *Hayride*; it was way before his time. He was just a kid when Elvis made his debut, a 13-year-old glued to the TV screen in Oak Grove, Louisiana, way up in the top right corner of the state — which places it even farther away from the best of the swamps as it did from the *Hayride* itself. But when the Gods of Rock History looked around for someone to blame for swamp rock, Tony Joe White's name was on the tip of everyone's tongue, which makes it all the more odd that we keep coming back to Elvis. The boy barely made it out of Memphis, after all; and, by the time he got round to cutting "Promised Land," he'd rarely make it out again.

So how come it's so damned good?

Because Elvis had stopped giving a shit, that's why. He didn't care what his record label said, he didn't care what the Colonel told him. On a bad day, and there were a lot of those, he didn't even care what his fans might think. But on a good day, the days when he remembered who and what he used to be, he shrugged all the bullshit and rubbish aside, and simply let rip like he knew he could. Sequestered at the Stax Studios in Memphis in the weeks before Christmas, with James Burton on guitar and David Briggs on organ, J. D. Sumner leading the chorus and Felton Jarvis on the boards, Presley literally seethed, spitting out a road map and laying his entire reputation on the line.

And why? Because he could; and, because every journey has to set out from somewhere, ours begins where Elvis' ended, 272 miles north of where we intended to start it, in Memphis, Tennessee. Highway 61 hits there, after all, and that's the road that we want to take, but it's something more than that as well. For, wherever you stand in the city, it's more or less a straight umbilical cord to the heart of Lauderdale Courts.

We are Mr. and Mrs. Author, as the owner of a Thibodaux motel renamed us when he learned of our quest. Dave and Amy to our friends. But you won't be seeing too much of us here. I hate those books where the traveling penman stops in every town to indulge in fascinating conversation with picaresque locals, whom he paints in your mind's eye like the cast of a prime-time sitcom: old Fred with the snaggletooth and a memory the length of the Arkansas River; Mrs. Wiggins at the grocery store, who can't tell you much about the reasons you came here, but knows everything else about everyone in town; Jacques, the weather-beaten Creole whose last nerve was shattered when the government built a cell phone tower three miles from his perimeter fence.

These people exist: I know because we met them. But you probably won't, mainly because very few of them really seemed that excited about having themselves preserved in print. They weren't hostile about it — nobody leaped from their seat and flounced out of the room, uttering dire imprecations and a pox upon my laptop — but, like the apocryphal fellow we met a few pages back, there was a very definite sense that they'd told me all I needed to know, and *if you need directions, maybe you don't have any business going there.*

Not everyone was reluctant, of course; in fact, some were encyclopedias, not only about their own lives, but a host of others as well. People like Calvin Newborn, for example, who is the reason we stopped in Memphis in the first place, and the reason why we even cared to look up Lauderdale Courts on the atlas.

We were lucky to find it; not because of any in-built obscurity — with the obvious exception of Graceland, Lauderdale Courts is the Memphis home where Elvis Presley lived the longest, from September 1949 to January 1953 — but because it very nearly fell prey to the wrecking ball.

In the mid-1990s, Presley's teenage home was scheduled for demolition, doubtless to make way for something really exciting that every city needs so badly, like condos or car parks. It took the concerted efforts of Memphis Heritage (a preservation organization), the City of Memphis, a couple of developers and a whole raft of fans to hold off the demolition squad — but Lauderdale Courts today stands proudly on the National Register of Historic Places, in its shiny new guise of Uptown Square. It remains a long way from anything that the Presleys would have recognized, but still the guides can point to the spot and tell you straight. *That's* where Ma and Pa Presley, Grace and Vernon, were living when their boy hit 16, desperately poor, but somehow always able to find the money to buy their precious son the most expensive gifts. Elvis, it is said, was regularly stuffed with all the food that he wanted, and even provided with silver table utensils. He might have been living in one of the direst housing projects in northeast Memphis, but when Elvis sat down to eat, he could have been dining with royalty.

His address, Apartment 328 at 185 Winchester Street, Memphis, Tennessee, certainly raised eyebrows amongst the Presleys' white friends. If it wasn't quite the ghetto, it was as near as you could get to it, and Earl Greenwood, Elvis' second cousin, once remembered his mother asking why the Memphis Housing Authority "couldn't place them [the Presleys] with their own kind," and adding, "I just hope our neighbors don't find out."

Elvis himself suffered even crueler taunts, both for his address — which, of course, he couldn't do much about — and for his appearance — which he could have, if he'd cared. He had recently got a new haircut, a strange lacquer-laden helmet-shaped job that sat precariously on his head, looking for all the world as though it were something he balanced there when he left the house every morning. Of course his classmates teased him about it, and usually he'd suffer their mockery in silence.

One day, though, another boy told him that the reason he lived on Winchester Street in the first place was because "he was so weird that only the niggers will let you live near them." Then he warned everybody else not to get too close. "Who knows what we'll catch?"

Elvis lashed out, in sheer fury, he later apologized, for the first time in his life. His tormenter went flying, a geyser of blood gushing from his nose and lip, and if the other kids hadn't stopped the brawl, who knows what Elvis would have done? Parted from his victim, however, Elvis merely patted that peculiar hair down and walked casually away. No one ever said anything about his address again.

Elvis' life at this time revolved around the Reserve Officers' Training Corps, probably the only organization at Hume High that hadn't objected to his hairstyle. Even the football team refused to let him try out unless he got it cut. He laughed them off, and though he was still considered "weird," now there was a buzz of respect going around. Elvis might not have had much going for him, but what he had he made certain he kept — and that included that helmet-shaped hairstyle.

He was also dressing in a way that few people around him even pretended to understand. He seemed to be a permanent fixture around the neighborhood thrift stores, thumbing through piles of discarded old clothes looking for anything that would catch the eye, and the gaudier the better. Resplendent in his newfound outfit, he would then strut proudly down the street, a startling blur of green and pink, stripe and polka dot. And, though he was staring straight ahead, apparently oblivious to everything around him, through the corner of each eye he would be reveling in the reaction he inspired, the shocked second glances he drew from the people he passed.

A regular haunt was Lansky Brothers, on Beale Street. It was the best, and by far the hippest, clothes store in the whole of Memphis, and, for Elvis, Lansky's was heaven on earth, rack after rack of vulgar, wildly tailored clothing. He couldn't afford to buy anything, of course, but it was fun simply looking, and besides, Gladys was a genius seamstress. Always ready to indulge her baby, Elvis could have come home with rags, and she'd have turned them into a three-piece suit. The only cloud on her horizon, as she repaired the gaping holes a previous owner had left in Elvis' latest lurid jacket, came when she thought of the places he went when he wore these clothes.

The Ellis Auditorium stood five blocks south from Winchester

Street, and, the moment he turned 16, Elvis would hike down there whenever he could, to take in the gospel shows that lasted from eight until midnight. The shows were as riotous as Elvis' clothes; indeed, that was probably where he first heard of Lansky's, standing painfully amongst the swaying, cheering, chanting crowds at the auditorium, vicariously aware that no matter how outlandishly he was dressed, the guy standing next to him was even wilder.

It was the music that moved him the most, though. "There's no other sound like it," Elvis once said. "It's sung from the soul, deep down, the way you're s'posed to. The best music is the kind you feel."

When I first read that remark, I underlined it in red ink. It's what this book is about.

For Elvis, no more or less than any other teenager growing up surrounded by Memphis' blues heritage, the heart of the city was WDIA, the South's first black-oriented radio station. Armed with a feeble 250 watt output, WDIA commenced broadcasting in October 1948, a month after the Presleys arrived in Memphis. It was barely a shout at the end of the dial, no competition for the mega-broadcasters that would soon be bellowing out of New Orleans, Nashville, Miami and more, with a roar that not only swamped the American South, it impacted the Caribbean as well.

No radio station in American history has ever had a greater impact on musical taste. A whole generation of future stars grew up listening to WDIA, and, according to Calvin Newborn, one of those future stars himself, "what they got out of it was certainly as valuable as any PhD in African-American studies."

Newborn is in his mid-seventies today, but when he talks (as he does a lot) or smiles (as he does even more), you can still see the young man looking out of his face. He played on B.B. King's first recordings, back when B.B. was a young man too, and honed his chops on Beale Street when R & B ruled the world. Then in the mid-1950s it was off to New York City, for a regular gig opening for Count Basie. Charles Mingus, Roy Milton, Ray Charles, Sun Ra and Hank

Crawford all called upon Newborn to play with them, and it's prob- ably safe to say that, if there was a jazz guitarist who was hotter than Newborn, the fire department must have put him out. He still plays guitar today, in and around his home in Jacksonville, Florida, but when he plugs in and roars, it's Memphis that's melting the dance floor, and it's to Memphis that his memory returns, to the earliest days of what would become rock, and the bright-eyed young acolytes — himself included — who would be hammering it into shape.

A PhD, you said?

Newborn nods, and continues his story. "Not only did these cul- tural pilgrims obtain unlimited exposure to both the secular and sacred music of the blacks through the raps of their 'professors,' wdia's disc jockeys, they also received an educational grounding in the humor and language of what was still an unknown, or at least undiscovered, culture."

The station's first recruit would also prove to be the archetype. Professor Nat D. Williams, known to generations of future Memphi- sians as "Nat Dee," had taught history at Booker T. Washington High, which initially prompted fears that he might prove too high- brow for the common folk. But the Professor's drive-time show, *Tan Town Jamboree*, swiftly established itself amongst wdia's most pop- ular shows. One could hardly go out during rush hour without hearing the latest R & B hits blasting from the passing car radios.

The next jock to come onboard was Maurice Hulbert Jr., a fast- talking raver with a showbiz background and an instinctive understanding of the hustler-style djs who dominated the north. Listening to his 100 miles per hour jock spiel one day, wdia owner Mr. Ferguson said, "Maurice, you talk so fast you oughta have a name that means speed. From now on you're gonna be 'Hot Rod Hulbert.'"

The name stuck, and soon Hulbert was working a three-a-day schedule at the critically understaffed station. Each show went on the air at a different hour, was aimed at a different audience, and demanded a different mood and rap. At eight in the morning, following Nat Dee's sunrise *Tan Town Coffee Club* show, Maurice Hulbert would go on the air with his gospel show, *Tan Town Jubilee*, hammering the joyous yelping of the Five Blind Boys of Mississippi, the Dixie Hummingbirds and the Mighty Clouds of Joy through the ether.

At three in the afternoon, Hot Rod would erupt into earshot, a chattering blur of hipster teletype in manic overdrive, the mile-a-minute emcee of the *Sepia Swing Club*. And at three in the morning, Maurice the Mood Man would drift soothingly into the early hours of a new day — smooth, sexy and intimate with all the housewives, maids and laundresses out there.

Elvis Presley absorbed it all. More than that, no sooner did he become famous than he was offering his support to the station. There was something magical about WDIA, a sense that, no matter how many miles, and how many cultures and prejudices, separated its listeners, they remained all part of one big family, living for the music.

Elvis certainly learned that from the radio, but his studies were not confined only to that medium. There was a period around 1950 when he would diligently show up every Wednesday and Thursday night to see the Finas Newborn Orchestra perform at the Plantation Inn, a highway club just a short walk across the Harahan Bridge in West Memphis.

Finas (Phineas) Newborn was one of the leading lights of the Memphis music scene; in later years his sons, Phineas Jr. and Calvin, would become equally crucial. Right now, though, the boys were simply Elvis' peers, and although the Newborns lived some way from the Presley home in the Courts, Junior and Calvin already knew about the white kid who lived in the projects. The way Newborn tells the story, most kids their age did.

Like Elvis, Junior and Calvin were part of that generation which was reaping the material benefits of its predecessor's depression-era poverty. Their parents, too, were poor, and throughout those difficult years before the Second World War, to make ends meet Finas worked as cook helper at Normal School (now the Memphis State University), and at the nearby Army Depot, as well as playing drums in bands at night. He insisted that their mom stay at home as a full-time mother, and between them, Newborn says, "They gave us the best things they could possibly afford."

Of course, one of these things was a love for playing music, and the instruments to play it on. The first time Elvis saw the Newborn brothers, they were onstage with their father's orchestra: Junior playing piano, trumpet and occasionally vibraphone; Calvin handling guitar, and sharing occasional trombone and vocal spots with Wanda Jones, the woman who later became his wife. The rest of the group featured Gene "Bow Legs" Miller on trumpet and vocals; Jewel "Bro' Bear" Briscoe and Moses Reed on tenor sax; Kenneth Banks on bass fiddle; and Bow Legs' brother Baby Ray, who danced and sang.

Together, the orchestra packed a visual punch as powerful as its sound. Finas Newborn constantly emphasized staying on top of all the new things that came out, and giving the audience a show — something to see as well as something to hear. Baby Ray made sure that, even when the rest of the group were playing their instruments, they still let rip with some effective dance steps.

Musically, says Calvin, "we could handle almost anything we were asked to play — popular standards, rhythm and blues, even some country and western. Every night we would be showered with requests, and if we didn't already know the song, Dad would go out the next day and find either the sheet music or a recording of the song. The next time we played, we'd be prepared." With Dad coaching the Newborn brothers, the Finas Newborn Orchestra left no stone unturned, musically or otherwise.

But it was tiring, even for musically inclined teenagers like the Newborn brothers. Having spent all day in the classrooms at school, from 10 P.M. until 2 A.M. they'd be playing live. Hardly surprisingly, Calvin would break the routine by cutting class and going to the band room. "I think the bandmaster, Mr. Mack (Professor W. T. McDaniel), was partial to me because of Junior, who was a year ahead of me and probably the most gifted student Mr. Mack ever had. Whether or not I was cutting class, he would always urge me to continue learning. He used to say that we needed to be at least three times better than other people, meaning white people, to be successful. Later, after Elvis struck it rich, I realized just how right Mr. Mack was."

As time passed, the Newborns grew accustomed to seeing Elvis at their shows, although no more than a dozen words passed between them a night. "He looked so striking, standing there in whatever garish costume he had magicked together from his thrift stores threads, that the first thing I would do when I walked out onto stage was scan the crowd in search of him."

One day, the owner of their regular haunt at the Flamingo Club, Clifford Miller, came up with the idea of a week-long series of shows called "Battle of the Guitars." Every night (and twice on Sundays), Calvin would stride out to joust with none other than Pee Wee Crayton, the author of the classic "Blues after Hours."

Pee Wee didn't stand a chance! On his home turf, Calvin was invincible, "playing my guitar like I was making love to a woman, and using the right body language while I did it. I really did excite audiences, especially the female half, and I think everybody around me noticed that, the more I put into my performance one night, the more women there'd be in the crowd for the next."

But there was someone else in the crowd who was getting excited by Calvin's act, someone he would never have suspected of coveting the crown that Pee Wee eventually left Calvin to wear.

"Every night during that tumultuous week, I could sense rather than see Elvis studying my moves, feel his eyes running over my body as I went through my show. He memorized every gyration, every thrust, every twitch, and in years to come, I would watch Elvis the Pelvis shaking onstage and wonder what poetic nickname the media might have coined for me had things only been different. Calvin really doesn't rhyme with anything!"

One night at the Flamingo, Elvis came walking straight up to the bandstand, something he had never done before. "Usually," Calvin laughed, "he just hung around the back, as unobtrusive as a white boy could be in a club packed with African-Americans. Only later, once everybody's attention had been drawn into the show, would he move up towards the front."

On this night, though, he stopped right in front of Calvin "and asked me if he could play my guitar. I looked across at Dad seated behind his drums. He nodded an okay, so I shrugged and handed my instrument to Elvis."

Still on the dance floor, Elvis turned to face the audience, to find every eye in the club glued to him. No one knew what this strange-looking kid, now with long, straight black hair and the freaky clothes, was planning, but Elvis had it all worked out. He roared out the opening line to a song, crashed out a spine-breaking guitar chord, and with his hips and legs shaking a mile a minute, he played the hottest guitar the room had ever heard.

"The rhythm Finas played had him locked up so tight he couldn't have gotten out if he'd wanted to," Newborn marveled. "But he didn't want to. The audience went wild, it felt as though the entire building was shaking along with them." Newborn said he still feels sick when he remembers white disc jockeys describing Elvis as a country artist. "By the time he had finished, he had wrecked the house . . . and taken my guitar with it. Every string on my instrument had been broken, and even as Dad fished a new set out of his pocket, I knew that this was one guitar battle I wasn't going to win.

"There was no such thing as rock 'n' roll in 1951, but there were simply no other words that could describe what he did that night at the Flamingo."

There was no such thing as swamp rock, either, but it sounds like he'd figured that out as well, an immortal twang and a lonely howl, broken dreams and soaring ambition. Electric soup and soupy eclecticism. Wild celebration and manic disturbance. Thunderclap rhythm and scratched-out blues. Glorious gospel and hillbilly growl. Presley wrapped them all up in his guitar playing, and when he unleashed that voice as well, three tones under sultry, and seething with primeval sex, he had a genre down pat before it had even been described.

Afterwards, Calvin looked around for his tormenter, but not for the last time in his career, Elvis had already left the building. But he didn't take a sweaty rhinestone cape and a limo full of minders with him; he took the dream of the music with which he would one day conquer the world. And though I probably won't mention swamp rock again, or at least for a very long while, it's important to let it keep rolling around in your mind. Because it's what we're looking for, in some very strange places.

TRACK TWO

"Baron Samedi" by 10cc
from the LP *Sheet Music* (London Records)
1974

*[Robert Johnson] was a terrible man with the women.
And I reckon he got himself one too many, down there in
Louisiana. This last one, she gi'n him poison in his
coffee and he died. Wasn't but twenty-one. Even the
church folks felt bad about it.*

Son House, to Alan Lomax, 1942

Straight down from Memphis, and straight across from Jackson,
Mississippi, we pulled into Tallulah, Louisiana, around three. From
there, we'd head on south to Vidalia, Georgia, then cross back over
the river and the state line too, to grab Highway 61 outside Natchez,
and catch a snatch of Dylan's mythology. But not tonight. Tonight,
we were looking for the blues, and was it instinct or simply good ear-
sight that washed us into a bar on Bayou Drive, just in time to see
Baron Samedi turn in our direction?

What did he see? A Brit and a northerner, blond and brunette,
I'm Dave and this is Amy, and hey, how do you do? The universal
language of the fresh-into-town first timers.

What did we see? A voodoo spirit. Well, to be brutally truthful,
and at the risk of spoiling what could have been an amusing anecdote, we saw a man dressed as a voodoo spirit. His name was Joe,

and he'd been togging up like this for the past five or six years, every time Mardi Gras rolled around and his annual trip to New Orleans began beckoning. But he liked to give his gear a dry run before the big day, so he'd be out on the streets of Tallulah, just to see how people reacted.

They usually stared in disbelief.

We noticed his outfit first. The white top hat, the black tuxedo, the dark glasses masking the eyes. His nostrils were plugged, his face was a skull. He could have been a corpse on his way to be buried, or he could have been a spirit raised from the dead. He was Samedi; he was Saturday; he was Cimitière; he was death. He was Papa Legba. He was whoever he wanted to be, and whoever you required him to be as well.

In voodoo ritual, Samedi is the spirit you call up first, and the one you bid farewell to last, for it is he who gives (or denies) the seeker permission to speak with the gods. And when you meet him at the crossroads, you stand poised between this world and the next.

Samedi is a master linguist, an able warrior and the personal messenger of human destiny. And, for those of us who weren't raised in voodoo tradition, you probably met him for the first time through the movies or music. He dances through James Bond's *Live and Let Die*; he makes a memorable appearance midway through the Pretty Things' seminal *S.F. Sorrow* LP; and he boasts about his prowess for a few exhilarating minutes of percussion and thunder on the second 10cc album . . . a man who walks on fire and doesn't get burned; who treads on glass and doesn't get cut; who can cure whatever ails you. And if you get it into your head to slit his throat, he probably won't even notice. But you probably shouldn't try.

Samedi is a man of many moods. One moment, he could be reeling drunk on rum and cigar smoke, stroking his cock and bellowing obscenities. But the next, he could be silent, patiently waiting at the end of your life to convey you to the realm of the dead. In bed he is neither man nor woman, unless he wants to be either or both, and in mixed company, he is the joker that you cannot shut up, rapid-firing off-color comments to whoever he knows will be most discomforted by them.

None of which explains why he's sitting across the table from us, doubtless wondering how the immortal personification of resurrection and sex ever came to be sharing a drink with two road-worn travelers, when he could be. . . .

"Samedi is a corruption of Semetye," Joe tells us, "which is what the folk round here call a cemetery. Every cemetery has its Baron, usually the first man who was buried there when the place was first dug, and the first woman is its Brijit, from Semetye's wife, Madam Brijit. And if you want to call him, you go to the cross that stands at that grave, and that's another of his names, Baron LeCroix. But you need a good reason if you're going to do that, because Samedi doesn't just come out for fun. Not for anything you'd consider fun, anyway." And all this in that heavily cadenced and slang-inflected singsong accent which other writers try to duplicate so phonetically, but which just doesn't look right on de printed page.

Voodoo itself is what a lot of out-of-staters believe to be the local state religion. The word itself was adapted from *vodun*, the Fon/Gbwe word for spirit, and it probably has more spellings than any other religion in the West. No matter. Voodoo, vodoun, verdun, whatever you want to call it, is a system of beliefs . . . or a religion . . . or a practical magical system . . . that spread out of Africa with the slave trade. There was never a single voodoo religion; rather, it is a mingling of several African tribal religions, all of which were aimed at permitting the slaves to maintain their relationship with the spirits, after they were snatched bodily out of the regions that the modern atlas calls Togo, Burkina Faso, Benin, Senegal and southern Ghana in the early 16th century, and washed up on the coasts of the Caribbean Islands and the New World.

There it took on a life of its own, and took over the lives that it found there already, mingling and merging with whatever other

On the edge of the bayou, a cypress tree grove is draped in moss.

belief systems were already in place — their new owners' Catholicism, mainly, but others, too; Santería in Cuba, Mandible in Brazil — and becoming a fresh law, and lore, of its own.

How did it reach Louisiana?

"Slowly," explains Joe, his measured voice seeming ever-so-slightly out of place behind the mask that marks his face. "First there was a revolution in Haiti, which shifted a lot of souls to Cuba. Then they were displaced from there, and they migrated to New Orleans, bringing their slaves, and their slave beliefs with them. And, because Louisiana was overflowing with French and Spanish Catholic influences, which had already become mixed up with earlier local and African beliefs, it strengthened and grew from there."

Voodoo is a religion, but it is also a way of life. Today it might seem easy to learn its secrets, from the classified ads in the back of any publication, the ones where the mysteries of voodoo ("powerful spells for love, money and power!) are on sale alongside mind-blowing condoms and ritual soap.

But step beyond the retarded enablement that is modern-day paganism, stop to think of what you are actually dealing with, rather than what the ad-men promise (if the money spells work so well, then why do they need to sell them to you in order to make a buck for themselves?), and voodoo steps beyond life itself. It is a force for healing and the power of protection. It is rite and might, it is love and death, and, in antebellum Louisiana, it was the knowledge that the slave owner might have controlled his slaves' bodies, but he could not control their minds, their instincts or their memories. Or the spirits, the Loa.

Samedi is just one of many Loa, but his interactions with man are so profound and varied that, even among nonbelievers or acolytes, he has stepped out of legend and into the modern world. Which is where Robert Johnson came across him.

Robert Johnson, to many minds, is the archetypal Southern bluesman. He was born in Hazlehurst, Mississippi, in 1911 . . . or maybe 1912, depending upon which of his biographies you believe. His father was a furniture maker who was chased out of town by a lynch mob when the boy was still a baby; Robert and his mother remained in Hazlehurst for a while, but then she sent the boy to live with his father in Memphis, and he back-and-forthed between his parents for much of his early life.

He wasn't an especially gifted musician, at least as a youth. Another bluesman, Son House, often spoke of his first encounters with the young Johnson, describing him as a scrawny kid who tried so hard to copy Son's technique, but could never quite get it right. And then the boy vanished off the face of the earth — and when he came back, he was the greatest bluesman of all.

The most legendary, too — a consequence of a short life, a shattering ability, and the sheer immediacy of the legends that have grown up around him. He sold his soul to the devil, they say, and the devil always takes what is his.

Except it wasn't the devil. It was Samedi who put Robert Johnson on the stage. Before they met, after all, Johnson was just a jobbing bluesman, no better or worse than any of his rivals. And then he took it into his head one night to mosey on down to the crossroads, to see what he could see.

There is a bucketload of variations on this one primal fact,

The moss gets everywhere; this is an oak grove.

although most of them place Johnson in the same menial career, a worker at the Dockery Plantation, a 10,000-acre cotton plantation and sawmill, perched on the Sunflower River between Cleveland and Ruleville, Mississippi. The crossroads were just down the road from there, and with midnight chiming as he reached them, Johnson was greeted by a large black figure.

"What do you want?" the figure supposedly asked.

"To play the blues," Johnson replied. "And play them better than anyone else."

The figure took his guitar and retuned it. Then he played a few tunes and handed it back, and Johnson's ambitions came true. And all they cost him was his soul.

He wasn't the first man to have made that exchange, not even in the annals of the blues. Clara Smith was singing "Done Sold My Soul to the Devil (and My Heart's Done Turned to Stone)" almost a decade before, in 1924. And Johnson may not have even done it at all. That doyen of Americana, Alan Lomax, shrugs the story of Johnson's pact aside, retelling it as merely a distortion of another belief entirely.

"In fact, every blues fiddler, banjo picker, harp blower, piano strummer and guitar framer was, in the opinion of both himself and his peers, a child of the devil, a consequence of the black view of the European dance embrace as sinful in the extreme."

But Johnson's tale was the one that flew the fastest, especially as his life was so short, and Samedi had to be the person he met, because who else could it have been? Right around the same time as Johnson was writing his songs, folklorist Harry M. Hyatt was scouring the South in search of legend, and learned from any number of interviews that, when people talked of going to the crossroads to make a deal with the devil, the Christian Satan was the furthest thing from their minds. Samedi was far smarter than him.

And that, says Joe, was that, and as for all the ethnographical explanations and studies that have sucked the life out of every legend you can think of, Joe just flicked an ash in the air, and took another drag on his cigar.

"People today, they can go to college now and learn culture and religion, and then they can sit down at their typewriter and tell the world what they think it all means, and they don't know jack shit between them. Because all their fine words don't make it true, and they probably don't even believe them themselves. Not deep down, which is the only place that matters," and a white-gloved hand was laid over his heart, as if to suggest that he might even have had one.

"Because that's where you'll find the only truth you need, underneath everything that you've been taught and told, and had crammed into your tiny mind by your TV and your preacher and your teachers and everyone else. It's the things that you hold so deep inside that even you aren't aware of a lot of them, those are the truths by which you live your life, and the only difference between an angel and a devil is that one of them is usually a lot more honest than the other."

Despite what Son House said at the beginning of this chapter, though, Robert Johnson, the king of the Delta blues, didn't really die in Louisiana. He wasn't even poisoned there. He met his end where his story began, in the heart of Mississippi.

On Saturday, August 13, 1938, the 27-year-old bluesman was playing a juke joint in the back room of Shaples General Store at Three Forks, on the outskirts of Greenwood, Mississippi.

Shaples is long, long gone today, and Three Forks is now just another intersection, where I-49 east runs into Highway 82. But that, it is said, is where a jealous husband laced Johnson's drink — a bottle of whiskey, rather than the cup of coffee that Son House thrust into lore — with either strychnine or lye. Johnson sickened; he was taken to a home in the Baptist Town section of Greenwood, and three days later he died. For cause of death, his death certificate noted, simply, "no doctor."

There's a scene in Mick Jagger's movie debut, *Performance*, which says everything you could ever want to know about Robert Johnson. It's not even a couple of minutes, because it's almost a throwaway compared to some of the other scenes in the film; it didn't make the soundtrack album, and there's probably nobody who ranks it high among Ol' Rubber Lips' greatest performances.

Regardless, the fractured medley of "Come on in My Kitchen" and "Me and the Devil Blues" that Jagger, as reclusive pop star Turner, scratches out on an acoustic guitar takes you out of the movie; out of the West London pad where the action is set, and out of yourself as well, to a tiny corner in your mind's darkest passageways, where your imagination is your only friend, and even it isn't sure whether or not it likes you. Sibilant and sinister, impassioned and paranoid, it reminds us (as if we needed reminding) why Johnson is considered one of the all-time greats — why his songs, his style, his very mannerisms, have been aped and appropriated by so many of rock's most storied names.

Eric Clapton described Johnson as "the most important blues singer that ever lived." Led Zeppelin, Jeff Beck and the Rolling Stones have all fed off his influence. Sitting back in our motel room later in the evening, rewatching *Performance* on a rented DVD machine, my wife and I realized that it didn't matter where Robert Johnson died. The fact is, he did. And it doesn't matter where you bury his body, his evil old spirit is still gonna ride the Greyhound bus. According to legend, that was always his preferred mode of transport.

You may not know this, but modern America was built on the Greyhound. The songs all say it was the railroads, and they have their place in the scheme of things, shunting their way from goods yard to goods yard, carrying the news as they passed through each town. But, for most of the past century, if somebody wanted to move from A to B as cheaply as possible and without watching the clock, it was the Greyhound that served their purposes.

They weren't known as such back then, but the first Greyhounds rolled out in 1914 from Hibbing, Minnesota; 45 years later, Bob Dylan would hitchhike out of the same town on his way to New York City. The company adopted the Greyhound name and logo in 1926, by which time its Swedish founder, Carl Wickman, either owned or franchised bus routes as far afield as California; according to company legend, it was one of Wickman's drivers, a man named Ed Stone, who came up with the name, after passing through a small town in northern Wisconsin and catching sight of another bus reflected in a store window. It reminded him, he said, of a greyhound.

By the time the company incorporated in 1929, Greyhound was already running a transcontinental service from California to New York City; less than a decade later, when Robert Johnson's mean old boneless bones first leaped aboard a passing vehicle, more or less the entire United States was being served by Greyhounds, with stations in over 4,500 different towns and cities. And, by 1968, when Paul Simon came to write "America," the song that sent the Greyhound name soaring into pop immortality, an entire generation of young Americans had taken advantage of the company's unlimited mileage dollar-a-day special offer, "99 days for $99." Robert Johnson didn't need to buy a ticket.

Where did he travel? Where didn't he travel would be a better question. His music and spirit hit the American North, to flavor the blues as they took root there. It crossed the ocean to haunt the Brits. It journeyed to Europe, Australia, Asia. Anywhere that the blues still live, Robert Johnson lives there too.

But Joe was growing restless. He didn't come here to talk about Robert Johnson, he told us. He came here to talk about Blind Joe Reynolds. So we listened.

TRACK THREE

"The Witch Queen of New Orleans" by Redbone
from the LP *Witch Queen of New Orleans* (Epic)
1971

Joe spoke of angels and devils. Well, Blind Joe Reynolds was one of the devils, and there's a story he told to prove it. One day, Reynolds was out and about — and it doesn't matter at this stage if you know who he was or not — "he was out and about, when he came across a woman sitting in a clearing in the woods outside of Tallulah, Louisiana. Now, if there was anything he liked more than making trouble, it was making love, so he makes a move on the woman, but she moves away. So he keeps on moving on her, and she keeps on moving away, until finally he lunges at her — and she vanishes with a flash of fire, and, for the first time, he sees what she'd been doing in the clearing in the first place. Lighting a fire, arranging the bones . . . he'd disturbed her at her work, and she cursed him to be disturbed forever. And you could say that everything bad that ever happened to Joe, it started happening then."

And who was that woman?

"It was Marie Laveau."

Hmmm. Somehow, I thought it might be.

If there's a voodoo legend in Louisiana, Marie Laveau is usually behind it. Not because she *was* behind it, but because she's the only

The only known portrait of Marie Laveau, the Witch Queen of New Orleans.

Voodoo Queen that the tour guides and the storytellers know that we out-of-towners might have heard of. And I do suspect that this is another instance of that, not only because the real Laveau died a good 19 years before Blind Joe was even born, but also because you have to wonder what the Witch Queen of New Orleans was ever doing all the way up in Tallulah in the first place.

Marie Laveau was born in New Orleans in 1794, one of the first children of the Haitian diaspora. Her father, a wealthy French-born plantation owner, fled the island with his family at the very outset of the revolution; her mother, an African, may have been a freed slave, and that freedom was retained by Marie.

She was beautiful, dark-skinned and darker hair, with eyes that reverberated mystery, and she knew how to use that beauty. She understood how her flesh shone when she stood in naked firelight, knew how her eyes glistened when she turned them straight towards you. Magic is so very much in the eye of the beholder, and Laveau knew exactly what she looked like.

She worked as a nurse for a spell, and one legend claims she attended the wounded at the Battle of New Orleans; according to another, she was employed at the New Orleans jail, where she would calm the spirits of prisoners awaiting execution by serving them her own specially prepared homemade gumbo.

She married young, as was the custom, but her first husband, Jacques Paris, died soon after, and nobody seems to know whether or not she wed Christophe Glapion, the man with whom she bore no fewer than 15 children — but one of these, her daughter Marie, would also become renowned as a highly skilled voodoo practitioner, often working alongside her mother to give the impression that Marie Laveau could appear in two places at the same time. The two women, apparently, looked very much alike.

Marie's greatest dramas, however, took place on the Bayou Lafourche, where she would enact vast public voodoo rituals, dancing with her pet snake, Zombi, calling down the elements and raising the waters, and pulling what cynical onlookers would describe as every conjuring trick in the book out of her hat, to impress the onlookers not only with her power, but also with the knowledge that, if they should ever need a Voodoo Queen, then she was one they should seek.

Great New Orleans Voodoo Kings and Queens

Sanite Dede

Marie Laveau

Marie Laveau II (daughter)

Doctor John

Joseph Melon

Doctor Beauregard

Doctor Jack

Doctor Yah Yah

Dr. John probably sings the best-known song about Marie, adapting it from an old jazz number, an ode to "a conjure lady" who "made a fortune selling Voodoo and interpreting dreams. . . ." But it was the Los Angeles–based rock band Redbone, led by the brothers (and the song's composers) Lolly and Patrick Vegas, who nailed her mystique, invoking her name in the song's darkly percolating opening refrain, "Marie, la Voodoo veau, she'll put a spell on you. . . ." Celebrating all the mystery with which a good folk legend should reverberate, in the space of just three minutes, "Witch Queen of New

Orleans" wrapped up everything: from the shack out in the swamps where she "stirred her witch's brew," and cultivated the tanna leaves that were "guaranteed to blow your mind," to that early morning in the "mucky swamp dew" when she "disappeared with hate in her eyes" — hounded out of town, we presume, by the locals, after one wild spell too many.

In fact, Marie Laveau died quietly at the age of 87, and was buried with full Catholic ceremony in Cemetery Number One in New Orleans — and, though the tourists still come to mark an X on her grave, in the hope that she will rise to their aid, it's just as likely that she rests peaceably. Because, though she may have been a healer, she was also a hairdresser; she may have been a witch, but she was also a devout Catholic, and, though her name is synonymous with voodoo magic, she was also a very good listener. Women would come to have their hair cut, and they would chatter while she worked, about themselves, about their friends and enemies, neighbors and who knew what else? Marie simply took what she learned and used it well.

Sometimes she could still people's fears with her magic alone; other times, she used her private knowledge. Asked, one time, to help the son of a prominent citizen to escape an open-and-shut murder rap, it is said that Marie simply placed a bag of herbs beneath the presiding judge's chair and bent his will to hers. It is just as likely, however, that she bent his ear too, passing on a piece of information that the worthy man would have preferred to remain secret, and letting him know that it would. For a price.

Blind Joe Reynolds paid a price, too, whether for disturbing one of Laveau's spectral rituals, or for the other crimes and sins that mounted up in the footprints he left behind him.

Eric Clapton and Cream may have guaranteed his immortality when they included his "Outside Woman Blues" on their mega-selling *Disraeli Gears* album in 1967, and if Reynolds was aware of the fact, it didn't affect his lifestyle. Or, due to the glacial nature of royalty payments, his income. And while Robert Johnson fans

Marie Laveau's grave is a magnet for her modern disciples.

bemoan the fact that their idol recorded just a handful of songs — if 29 different titles, and 42 performances, can be counted as a handful — they're lucky. Blind Joe recorded even fewer, eight to be precise, and two of those have never been heard since the day that they were recorded, or at least since the master tape vanished, which probably wasn't very much later.

As for the rest, the other half dozen; well, they were all blues, of course, a Delta howl littered with the dialect of the region. He sings of "stringarees" and mourns "a big fat mama with meat shakin' on the bone." He admonishes women for wearing short "nehi" (or knee-high) dresses, and warns married men how to keep their ladies in check (buy a bulldog, "cos women these days get so doggone crooked"). And he's so sick of eating chicken, he hears clucking in his sleep.

"Outside Woman Blues," "Nehi Blues," "Ninety-Nine Blues" and "Cold Woman Blues" were cut for the Paramount label; "Third Street Woman Blues," "Married Man Blues," "Goose Hill Woman Blues" and "Short Dress Blues" were recorded for Victor, and half of them weren't even recorded under his best-remembered name. He was also Blind Willie Reynolds, although his real name was

SUPERSTITION, DEPRAVITY AND LUST LOCKED ARMS.
CORRECT PICTURE OF THE VOU-DOU DANCE DOWN TOWN ON TUESDAY!

A 19th-century vision of a suitably depraved Vou-Dou dance. "Lust Locked Arms!" This appeared in the New Orleans Mascot *newspaper in 1889.*

apparently either Joe Sheppard or Joe Leonard, and he wasn't blind until his mid-twenties, when he fell into an argument with a friend named Brudell Scott, and was blasted straight between the eyes with a shotgun full of scattershot.

He should have died, but didn't. He did lose his eyesight, though — hell, he lost his eyes as well, and a lot of the skin around them, too. There are only a couple of photographs of Reynolds in existence, and they both look like something out of a horror film, but the weird thing is, that seemed to suit him just fine. Blues historian Gayle Dean Wardlow wrote what passes best for Blind Joe's biography, a few pages in his epic recounting of the music's origins, *Chasin' That Devil Music*, and more or less the first time we even meet the man, it's in the words of Jack Brown, a store-owner remembering the future legend's childhood, in the shacks and back streets of Tallulah, not too many decades after the city was founded.

"There's a story there," Joe (the Joe that we've met) interrupts softly. "Back in the days when the railroads were coming, they had all sorts of routes planned out for it, but there was one little old lady in these here parts, who really fancied a railroad line running across her plantation. So she gets hot and heavy with the railroad contractor, and convinces him that the only route that really made sense was the one that she wanted, because that was the one that led to her bed. So he falls for her and falls for her line, and he builds the railroad just where she wanted it, at which point she cut him dead and never spoke another word to him, and left him so broken-hearted that he cut her back instead. He'd promised to name the stop for her plantation. Instead he called it for an old sweetheart of his, named Tallulah."

Today . . . well, today Tallulah is best known as the first city in America to open a shopping mall — which is a little like taking pride in the fact that you were the first person to scratch an antique armoire; and, before that, there was that nasty business with the goat.

"You see, the local doctor shot a goat, and got into a fight with its Sicilian owners," Joe says. "Well, nobody liked the Sicilians back then, so the locals all sided with the doctor, of course. The Sicilians were lynched, and the law did nothing, and when somebody asked them why, the sheriff just shrugged. Because there was no way on earth that he could arrest every white man in Madison County."

That was in 1899. The following year, Joe Sheppard (later Reynolds) came along; a few years after that he had that meeting in the clearing, and Tallulah was never the same again.

"Anything 'bad' was Joe," Jack Brown told Gayle Dean Wardlow. "Yes sir; anything 'bad' was Mister Joe . . . Joe was somethin'! He's a devil of a Joe." A devil that was so darned wicked that, by the end of his life, he couldn't even tell his best friends precisely what he'd done. He just let them guess why the law was on his trail, why he kept on changing his name, why he never stayed still for any longer than he had to. But there were rumors, of course. One was that he shot his own uncle. Another was that he murdered a white man. Another, and this is the one that he told his death certificate, was that he didn't even come from Louisiana, that Arkansas took the blame for raising him.

But no, Reynolds was a Tallulah boy, growing up within spitting distance of the river, and proud to run riot whenever he could. And if there was mischief to be done, or even to be found, he'd usually be at the front of the pack, whether rolling passersby for whatever loose change he could scavenge, or else dreaming up more elaborate stunts, taking them out to the banks of Catfish Lake, and charging them money to sit with him and wait for the bloody skeleton that haunted those waters to rise up and scare them half to death. The skeleton never showed up, but some of Reynolds' friends would, and they were scary too.

Maybe that's why he got out of town whenever he could, even flitting across the river to Vicksburg, Mississippi, when the heat was on, and the only thing that kept him out of even more trouble was the fact he was already strumming a mean guitar.

A guy named Hey Willie — because that's what people shouted when they saw him — was Reynolds' first teacher, Hey Willie and a fiddler whom everyone called Deaf John. Maybe because he was. But Blind Joe Reynolds outshone them all, and, even before he started playing for cash in Vicksburg, he was taking trips out to Kansas-Kansas — not the city or the state, but a godforsaken hole on the railroad tracks where the rail men gathered for rotgut and girls.

There, Reynolds would serenade them through whatever other fascinations kept a crowd in one place, and though he never collected a wage for his work, there were plenty of tips, and a load of perks, too. That same Tallulah buddy who told writer Grayson the rest of Reynolds' story made it clear that the young man was a remarkable womanizer. "He tried to get all the women he seed and all that they had."

He wasn't a religious man, either. "Never knew Joe to go to church much. If he did, he'd be off from the church arguin' and cussin' and raising sand." Even as he grew into adulthood, there was, apparently, "much devilment" in store when Joe was on the prowl.

That prowling came to an abrupt end in the early 1920s, when a posse rode in from out of town, and carted Reynolds off to jail. He'd done something or other, no one knew what, on one of his trips into Arkansas, and the local powers that be had tracked him down. He was thrown into a cell, and there he stayed until the last day of his sentence was done. Then he went back to Tallulah, and he fell into a whole new heap of hurt. He was blinded.

"They's drinkin' and got drunk and got to cussin' and arguin'," is how Jack Brown recalled it. "One broke to get his gun, and the other 'un had his gun hid out there at the edge of the woods; he went and got his gun. And he's hidin' behind a tree . . . and Joe happened to peep out too quick. When they carried Joe to the hospital, and Joe got healed up where he could kinda get about, Joe left there." He had made too many enemies in Tallulah, he said, for him to hang around there any longer. He needed to get out to someplace where nobody hated his guts . . . and where he could learn to shoot unsighted.

It doesn't sound like anyone ever put him to the test, but one of Blind Joe's boasts was that he could shoot as well as any sighted man, just from letting his ears do the seeing. But he once shot a dog for worrying his shoelaces, and our Joe reckoned there were other killings, too, only no one ever saw enough to be sure that the blind man committed them. "Why, sure he had a gun, and sure he was happy to wave it about. But whoever heard of a man with no eyes taking down a moving target from the other side of the bar?"

Where did he do his boasting? It might be easier to ask where he didn't. Mississippi bluesman Skip James saw Blind Joe playing in a cabaret in Memphis in 1926, and then busking on the streets of Sun, Louisiana, just a couple of months after that. He was in Clarksdale for a time, not only playing guitar, but also a clay jug that he used like a tuba. Or so it was said.

Bo Carter heard him performing someplace, and he put the word about. So did Charley Patton. So did Son House. So, while Reynolds raised a little more money by teaching bottleneck guitar, when his "big break" came, or what passed for such a thing, he was playing out at a sawmill barrelhouse, somewhere in the region of Lake Providence, way the hell up on the Arkansas state line.

There, the legendary blues-catcher H. C. Speir — the man who would one day discover Robert Johnson — finally followed up on the reports he'd been getting from his musician friends around the area, and journeyed out to hear Reynolds perform. Just weeks later, in February 1929, Blind Joe Reynolds was off to Grafton, Wisconsin, where he cut four sides for the Paramount label in nearby Port Washington.

Paramount was a serious blues label. Skip James, Charley Patton, Blind Lemon Jefferson, Blind Blake and Son House all recorded for Paramount, and blues fans agree it was the best of the best. At the time, though, the label could barely give its music away. The Great Depression was raging, and, frankly, people had better things to spend their money on than a fragile 78. Plus, the blues were such a minority interest that, even with all the cash in the world, most people had no interest in the animal yowlings of a few scratchy Southerners.

"Outside Woman Blues"/"Nehi Blues" was released in early 1930, and this one did sell sufficient copies for Paramount to put out a follow-up. But "Ninety Nine Blues"/"Cold Woman Blues" didn't sell a bean. Nobody knows how many Paramount moved, but they certainly know how many survived, and the answer to that was one. One copy of the record is known, and that only turned up in the year 2000. It's now the property of record dealer and collector John Tefteller, whose website tells the story of its discovery:

> *Bruce Smith, a school teacher from Ohio with an appreci-*
> *ation for old blues records, was attending a teachers'*
> *conference in Nashville. With an hour to kill before catching*
> *a flight home from a school conference, he wandered into*
> *the Nashville Flea Market and found the record in a stack*
> *of old 78s. The records were without sleeves and not in par-*

ticularly good condition, but the price was right at $1.00 each. He purchased three records – two were common blues records of the 1930s and the third was the long lost Blind Joe Reynolds. Unaware of its value, he purchased it simply because it "looked interesting." Tefteller would pay $5,500 for it.

"Sometimes songs can be long lost for good reason – they are not very good and didn't sell well because of it," Tefteller declares. "But not so in this case – this is a GREAT record. Reynolds plays a mean slide and really mumbles his way to immortality on 'Cold Woman Blues' [the b-side]. The significance of this record is mind-boggling! It may not be as important to blues history as finding the long lost Son House Paramount recording of 'Clarksdale Moan,' but it's real close!"

Well, now say, cold woman, is your clothes all clean?
The reason I ask is, you smell like pork and beans.
"Cold Woman Blues"

Reynolds cut four more tracks in Memphis around the same time as "Ninety Nine Blues" was lost to the world — the aforementioned "Third Street Woman Blues," "Married Man Blues," "Goose Hill Woman Blues" and "Short Dress Blues." The first pair became his next release, the latter two promptly disappeared from view and have never been seen or heard of again. And that was the end of his recording career. He would live another 40 years; he would be raised to legend by "Outside Woman Blues." But he never even heard the Cream record, and, though he carried on playing, and begging and sinning and everything else, his biggest gig for a long time was Jack Brown's grocery store in Monroe, Louisiana.

Occasionally his nephew, Henry, would take him out to Shreveport, Greenville, Natchez or Jackson, where he'd plug his new electric guitar into a tiny battery amp, and play on the streets for whoever cared to hear him. Perhaps he was in Shreveport the day that an inexplicable hail of peaches rained down on July 12, 1961. It was the kind of mischief he'd have enjoyed, after all. But when he died from pneumonia on March 10, 1968, most of the people who registered his passing didn't have a clue who he was, or who he'd once been . . . the greatest bluesman Louisiana ever spawned, and the voice that drops the "you" into bayou. There may not have been a drop of swamp in Blind Joe Reynolds' veins, but where other bluesmen shiver prairie and plantation, his very way of singing shifts the dust bowl from your dreams, and sends you somewhere darker, far darker. . . .

And that, concluded our evening's host, is why "you need to put Joe in your book. Because he was the biggest, baddest, blindest bluesman of the lot."

TRACK
FOUR

"Highway 61 Revisited" by Bob Dylan
from the LP *Highway 61 Revisited* (Columbia)
1965

Natchez, Mississippi, has so many claims to literary, musical, cinematic and cultural fame that it's either scarcely worth stopping in, or a place to spend the rest of your life.

It's when you leave the city limits that it really opens your eyes, though. Making an early start after the late night before, my wife and I barely noticed as we passed the shopping center and the parkways and the drives, the community hospital, and that last gasp flurry of retail expanse, all you can eat at Berry's Seafood, caps you can wear at Bad Boy Enterprises. But then we hit Mammy's Cupboard, and we knew that we were in the presence of genius.

Mammy's Cupboard is a gift store and coffee shop. It is also situated within the voluminous skirt of a 28-foot-tall black woman.

It's a reminder of the days when America had yet to give way to the leviathan of commerce: when stores had character and were owned by characters, too, rather than faceless drones who all worship Mr. Mart, and whose entire future in the retail trade seems to depend upon ensuring you don't use more carrier bags than you genuinely merit.

The boom for such building was on the eve of the Second World

War. Mammy's Cupboard's been here since 1940, and she's had good years and bad — good years when her clothes are all tidy, and her colors are bright; bad ones when time and weather have ruffled her folds, her paint job peeling. There was even a period when she only had one arm, and that was cut off at the elbow — shades of Amos Moses before we even get to the swamp.

Now she's intact again, and she holds out a tray to any passing trade, and yeah, there's probably some Political Correctolytes who wish the rest of her had crumbled to dust years ago, and that the eyesore was erased before the repairmen came back. But Mammy stands despite them, and if she doesn't sell the best hummingbird cake in the country, then she must have a sister that she keeps mum about.

Hummingbird Cake

3 cups flour
1 teaspoon baking soda
1 teaspoon salt
2 cups sugar
1 teaspoon ground cinnamon
3 large eggs, beaten
1 cup vegetable oil
1 1/2 teaspoons vanilla extract
1 8-ounce can crushed pineapple
1 1/2 cups chopped pecans
2 cups chopped banana
cream cheese frosting

Combine flour, baking soda, salt, sugar and cinnamon in a large bowl; add eggs and oil, stirring until moist. Stir in vanilla, pineapple, 1 cup pecans, and bananas. Pour batter into three greased and floured 9-inch round cake pans. Bake at 350 degrees for 25 to 30 minutes or until a wooden pick

inserted in center comes out clean. Cool in pans on wire
racks 10 minutes; remove from pans, and cool on wire racks.
Spread frosting between layers and on top and sides of cake;
sprinkle with ½ cup chopped pecans.

We were into the wilderness now, mile after mile of unchanging
green. Occasionally a road will splinter away to the side heading
somewhere, or a clump of houses will loom out of the verdancy, gallantly holding back the encroaching (or encroached upon) trees. But
you're as likely to see nothing as anything to look at, and the occasional tumbledown blur in the windshield reminds you that it's been
like this for decades.

The atlas calls it U.S. Route 61, but it's Highway 61 to the rest of
us, or the Blues Highway to the musically inclined. Fourteen hundred miles of tarmac that wind from Wyoming, Minnesota in the
north, all the way down to New Orleans, follow the course of the
Mississippi and, therefore, the first steps of the blues, out of the
South and up to the cities. Danny Adler — Cincinnati-born guitarist
with London's legendary Roogalator, and still one of America's
hottest blues guitarists — is an engine driver today, and, whenever
he crosses Highway 61, he lets out a lonesome whistle as a tribute to
its heritage.

Vicksburg, Mississippi; Memphis, Tennessee; West Memphis,
Arkansas; St. Louis, Missouri; Davenport, Iowa; Saint Paul,
Minnesota . . . this is the journey that so many names took, by thumb
or Greyhound or any other locomotion, and the highway used to go
on for another 314 miles from Wyoming, all the way to Duluth,
Minnesota, which might be another reason for its fame.

In 1965, while the back end of the route was still open (it was
decommissioned in 1991), Duluth-born Bob Dylan named his album
after the road, and peopled its title track, "Highway 61 Revisited,"

with such a panoply of colorful characters that you just knew he'd been watching the motors flow past him for decades.

God, Abraham, Georgia Sam, Mack the Finger, Louie the King . . . any one of these icons might have roosted by the roadside, one thumb stuck out to hitch a ride someplace. And there's a school of thought that reckons you can tug the song's geography from those names, in which case Louie the King must be the southernmost tip of the journey.

Highway 61 ends in New Orleans, "where the land of a continent," wrote journalist Ed Vulliamy, "dapples away into the ocean." What a beautiful image that is, one for the *National Geographic* supplements before they got groovy and truncated their brand. But it's not quite accurate. In fact, the road halts in the heart of the metropolis' concrete miasma, where Tulane Avenue smacks into South Broad Street, in front of the Orleans Parish Criminal Court. How many felons, over the years, have gone to face justice down the road that Dylan sang about?

There, Highway 61 loops onto Route 90, but those last few miles have another name — the Airline Highway, and not because it sails in a straight line from the Louis Armstrong New Orleans International Airport to the Baton Rouge Metropolitan Airport. No, Governor Huey P. Long built it long before then, beginning in the 1930s as a bypass for the older, winding Jefferson Highway, to create instead the straightest possible route from the capitol building in Baton Rouge to the bars and brothels of the Big Easy.

The legislators needed someplace to go in between drafting new laws and minding their civic duties, and the new road made certain that they didn't waste time getting there. Any reputation that this stretch of highway boasted back then has only been amplified in the years that followed. It was on Airline Highway in 1987 that Jimmy Swaggart was nabbed by rival televangelist Marvin Gorman, as he left the Sugar Bowl Courts Motel with a hooker. Gotcha!

Dylan was not the first songwriter to immortalize the highway in his music. Mississippi Fred McDowell's "61 Highway" and James

"Son" Thomas' "Highway 61" both got in there before him, and there's legend aplenty as well. Bessie Smith died on Highway 61; Elvis Presley grew up alongside it; Robert Johnson sold his soul to Samedi there, at the crossroads where it meets Highway 49.

"A lot of great basic American culture came right up that highway..." author Robert Shelton told the BBC, "and as a teenager, Dylan had traveled that way on radio.... Highway 61 became, I think, to him a symbol of freedom, a symbol of movement, a symbol of independence and a chance to get away from a life he didn't want...."

Certainly that is the role that Highway 61 plays in the song, as each verse plays out a problem that can only, or ultimately, be solved by heading down the road. In the first verse, God tells Abraham to kill his son. "Where should I do it?" asks Abe. "Out on Highway 61," replies his maker.

In the second verse, Georgia Sam is turned away by the welfare department, but told that he can find what he needs "down on Highway 61." In the third verse, Louie the King advises Mack the Finger how and where to dispose of a pile of junk; in the fourth, a woman complains to her father that her complexion is too white, and he tells her how she can fix the problem, and in the fifth, a bored gambler is looking for a suitable venue for the Third World War. Highway 61 is the answer to all of their questions.

In the British *Guardian* newspaper, Ed Vulliamy suggests that Dylan chose Highway 61 for his song because "it was such a quintessential slice of the American Midwest, along which life was stable and looked unlikely to change much." Maybe he did, maybe he didn't, although certainly by the time you get this far south, things have changed beyond all recognition, and even God would have a hard time getting anything done.

According to Alan Lomax, there was a time when there were only three sounds you'd hear as you motored down Highway 61. You'd hear a paddle steamer whistling for a landing, you'd hear a locomotive howling up a grade, and you'd hear a Greyhound bus blaring its

LA-7   *Beautiful Southern Home*

Louisiana's antebellum past rises up.

horn. Not now. The whistles are silent, the howls all seem computerized, and the traffic's going so slow half the time that if you want to actually hear — or even see — anything beyond your fellow motorists, and a stream of tankers, trucks and motorized monoliths, you have to leave Highway 61 a little before you leave Baton Rouge, and make for South River Road instead....

This route becomes River Road before too long, because that is exactly what it is. River Road hugs the Mississippi like a teddy bear, and it weaves through a landscape that is neither here nor there. On the one hand, Louisiana's antebellum past rises up in the form of the mansions and estates that once marked out the wealthy; on the other, the state's modernity pocks the landscape to indicate where today's money comes from, the Fortune 500-ers who have been raping the soil for so long that Mother Nature herself now has Stockholm syndrome.

Think of a company that was built up by chemicals, and their logo is probably here, monster steel and rusted metal, cranes the size of middling skyscrapers, pipes that extend like vast metallic tentacles, flames that blaze as bright as the sun. It's like something out of *Blade Runner*, if Harrison Ford had picked sugarcane, because the fields here are as lush as their surroundings are barren, and the weird thing is, for all the environmentalists' protests about industrial pollutants, it was only a century ago that the air around here would be so thick with smoke that you wouldn't even be able to breathe, let alone watch the farmers burning off the stubble of their crops, in readiness for the next year's planting.

We were practically atop the levee now, and every so often a sign would rise up, inviting us to leave River Road, to cut off one of the long loops of land that keep the Big Muddy firmly in their sights, and rocket off down a shortcut. Martin Luther King Parkway loomed and veered left a few miles back, but we stuck to the straight road, and, sure enough, there it was again, standing around on the corner to ask if the scenic route was as scenic after all. Or was it just another tangle of industrial forestry, the same as we'd be sick of seeing by the time we'd completed the journey?

The mind meanders back a century or so. If there is a sign that welcomes you to Carville (which was named before there were any cars at all), then we didn't see it. But still the town has its own claim to fame staked into the history of America, as the one-time home of the nation's first (and only) federally run leper colony. U.S. Public Health Services Hospital #66 is a museum now, among other things.

In its prime, the hospital looked more like a small rural college campus than a place of exile for the sufferers of a ghastly disease. Over two miles of covered walkways were laid out across the hospital grounds, to connect the offices to the infirmary, the chapels to the residences, the recreation center to the kitchens; John Tayman, author of *The Colony*, described the entire place as glittering with "ranks of neat dormitories, and greenswards, and well-maintained administrative buildings." The Daughters of Charity of Saint

Vincent de Paul played a major role in the hospital's running, and "nuns in blue-and-white habits pedaled three-wheeled bicycles down gravel paths and patients steered golf carts to the course."

Like so many of the grandest properties in the area, Carville started life as a plantation. A Virginia-born planter, Robert Coleman Camp, purchased the land from the government in May 1825, an old Houma Indian hunting and fishing ground, which he transformed into Woodlawn Plantation. And transformation is the right word. Where once there stood just barren wilderness, New Orleans architect Henry Howard placed the mansion that would become the centerpiece of the plantation; the same man was responsible for many of the finest estates that already ran up Great River Road, and it's doubtful that he ever dreamed that this particular commission would one day house the administrative buildings of a leper colony.

But the plantation withered, as such places often did, and in 1894, the Louisiana State Legislature took over the now-abandoned landscape and offered Dr. Isadore Dyer, the future dean of Tulane University Medical School, the chance to fulfill one of his life's ambitions, to establish the Control Board for the Louisiana Leper Home. It would be, the official order decreed, "a place of refuge, not reproach; a place of treatment and research, not detention."

It was not an easy task. Disease was rife in 19th-century Louisiana — some of it relatively mild, merely bothersome, like the dengue that laid low visitors to the state, but which scarcely worried the locals. But others cared nothing for your point of origin; did not even stop to ask whether or not you had acclimatized to the region. They laid you low regardless — not just leprosy, but yellow fever too.

The last outbreak of that plague, in 1878, had killed over 4,000 people in New Orleans alone. With many people predicting Yellow Jack's imminent return (correctly, as it happens, there was another massive outbreak in 1897), any suggestion that some kind of hospital was about to be built so close to some of the grandest homes on River Road was guaranteed to cause a stink — and again, the mood of the day bore some grim portents. In New Orleans, during the 1897 epidemic, plans to convert the Beauregard Public School on Canal Street into a hospital roused the local residents to arson.

Dyer, therefore, let it be known that he was building an ostrich farm, nothing more, and although that certainly raised a few eyebrows — what did you farm the ostrich for? — the locals let him get on with it. Especially after they were warned that prying eyes would probably be pecked out by the vicious birds. By the time they realized his true intentions, it was too late to do anything but watch.

In fact, if any place in the United States needed a home for its luckless lepers, it was Louisiana. The disease was shockingly common in the 18th and 19th centuries, and its sufferers tended to migrate to New Orleans, because at least there they had a chance of living longer, if only by the kindness of strangers. Kindness, however, was a double-edged sword. Ostracized by fear, disgust and apathy, the sufferers clustered wherever they could, until finally Governor Bernardo de Gálvez (who served from 1777 to 1785) could stand to hear of their existence no longer, and announced that henceforth all lepers were to be confined to a patch of wilderness close to the Bayou St. John, *la terre des Lépreux*, or Lepers Land.

A little more caringly, his successor, Governor Esteban Rodríguez Miro, then established a hospital in the same area very soon after his inauguration. For obvious reasons, the local, healthy, populace loathed its presence, and the hospital survived any number of attempts to burn it to the ground. Within 50 years, however, other, even more efficient solutions to the leprosy problem had apparently been arrived at, most of which seemed to involve either waiting for death or arranging an exile, and the hospital fell out of use. In 1833, perhaps appropriately, New Orleans Cemetery Number Three was constructed on part of its site.

Leprosy remained, however, and the first patients arrived at the Louisiana Leper Home immediately upon its completion in the mid-1890s, five men and two women who were brought in by barge from

New Orleans because no other form of transportation, steamship or railroad, would allow them to board.

Over the next decade, the colony grew slowly but surely. In 1905 the state took over its operation and began constructing many of the amenities that still stand today. In 1917, Senate Bill 4086 permitted the federal government to purchase the site, for $35,000, as the country's sole National Leprosarium. It opened under federal auspices in 1921, and, across the United States, a sigh of relief was heard as the individual states disgorged their own leper colonies into its care. Penikese Island, Massachusetts, for example, loaded its 13 sufferers, two women and 11 men, onto a tugboat to New Bedford (as, according to the local press, "the morbidly curious . . . gathered around"), where they boarded a hospital train to Louisiana.

Others found their way into the leprosarium through more grotesque means. Neil White, author of *In the Sanctuary of Outcasts* (2009), tells of one of the patients, an old woman named Ella, who contracted leprosy "at the age of 12. In 1926, a man the locals called the bounty hunter tried to take her from her one-room schoolhouse and transport her to the leprosarium at Carville. I'll never forget Ella repeating what a little boy in her classroom said: 'Oooh, Ella, the bounty hunter fixin' to carry you away.'"

Ella had good reason to fear these words. Leprosy was a life sentence, and so was Carville. Once incarcerated within its walls, she would lose her right to vote; to consort with the opposite sex; to mail a sealed letter; to receive visitors; to leave the 320-acre compound. Neither was Neil White's introduction to the leprosarium exactly conventional. Although the disease has never been fully eradicated (it is currently estimated to affect around 200,000 people in the United States, with around 100 or so fresh cases every year), the leprosarium's population declined as medical science grew more adept at preventing the spread of leprosy — or Hansen's disease as it has become more soberly, if less dramatically, known. By the early 1990s, there were no more than 130 sufferers in residence, a statistic which

prompted the Bureau of Prisons to begin transferring federal convicts to the colony to fill all those empty spaces. Neil White, sentenced to 18 months imprisonment for financial misdoings, was one of them, and his memoir chokes on the horror and outrage he experienced when he was told precisely where he'd be doing his time. It's a wonderful book.

The leprosarium has gone now, relocated to Baton Rouge in 1999. According to White, "the buildings were sold to the National Guard of Louisiana to use for juvenile delinquents," but around 20 of the patients refused to leave. "[So] they let those patients live in an isolated corner. Sixteen patients still live there; one just turned 100." Of the rest, the museum stands to remind us of their lives and deaths, and the only disappointment is that it's closed on Mondays.

Instead, we park and look out at the river, watching the oil tankers head up towards Baton Rouge, a Babel of exotic names and flags to remind you that these are considered international waters, even if their backwash is destined for some of the most parochial townships in America, tiny communities that cling to the riverbank, oblivious to the industry that can blot out the sun if you look closely enough.

Places like Killona, on the other side of the river. Many years ago,

LM 4   Cutting, Shocking and Stacking Sugar Cane in Louisiana

8A-H3253

A pre–WWII postcard depicting sugarcane-picking on one of Louisiana's great estates.

on a farm just outside town, there lived a woman named Matilde. For as long as anybody could recall, one of her neighbors would pasture his horse on her land, but one day Matilde refused him permission to do so. The next day the horse boldly walked onto her property, so she threw a stone at him. It struck him on the nose, and the beast fell dead.

Outraged, the horse's owner put a curse on her, declaring that she should never receive a moment's privacy or rest. Immediately, Matilde's home was filled with ghosts, who tormented her from dawn to dusk and all night as well, moving the furniture, breaking the crockery and beating her black and blue. She fled the house, and they followed her into the fields, still beating and abusing her, and all the while they kept up the refrain "Our master told us to move in here. You get out, Matilde."

But Matilde would not get out, and so finally the ghosts told her that if she continued to disobey them, she would be dead by

Christmas. And she was. That morning, a passing neighbor discovered her cold and stiff in her bed.

The house fell to ruin after that. Other families tried to move in, but the ghosts quickly chased them out again, and when a spiritualist group tried to take over the place, the angry spirits threw their benches into the air and tore their Bible to shreds. The spiritualists fled, and the house was left to decay away. If its foundations still stand, they are unmarked and unremembered, but the story still turns up in Louisiana ghost gazetteers, and that's good enough for us.

We pass through Marchland, just before the River Road is transformed into the more officious-sounding Route 44. Lutcher, Gramercy, Garyville . . . the map is growing crowded now, and so is the landscape — towns that may or may not have grown up to feed the factories, but are certainly in their thrall now.

Reserve, Louisiana, was once home to the largest sugar refinery in the United States. Parts of William Friedkin's *Bug* were filmed in New Sarpy, at Migliore's Grocery and the Boomerang Bar. Miss Teen USA 2004 came from Destrehan. Jazzman Kid Ory hailed from LaPlace, and if you think Norco sounds like something out of an industrial gazetteer, you'd be right; it was named for the New Orleans Refining Company, and any history it may have had before then — being the center of the German Coast Uprising of 1811, for example — is well buried beneath its new identity. Well, it was only the largest slave insurgency ever to take place in the United States.

The uprising lasted three days and took 30 minutes to suppress. Ninety-five slaves were killed either during the revolt or in its so-bloody aftermath, although the legislature of the Orleans Territory very kindly paid the planters $300 compensation for each slave killed or executed — almost one-quarter of whom, incidentally, had their heads lopped off their bodies, to be either placed on pikes and exhibited around the neighborhood plantations, or to decorate the New Orleans city gates to douse any other thoughts of rebellion.

Those gates, were they still standing, would be coming into sight now, although the point where the city begins and all else ends is difficult to discern any longer; one main drag looks much the same as any other, and if a city can be said to possess a unique character, something that makes it stand out on its own, you're not going to find it on Route 44, Highway 61, or any of the other roads that pull you into New Orleans — which is a shame, because there must be more to local dining than another polystyrene pack filled with lightly warmed cow.

Jambalaya, for example.

TRACK
FIVE

"Big Bad Moon" by Joe Satriani
from the LP *Flying in a Blue Dream* (Legacy)
1989

Thibodaux, Louisiana, was very different 40, 50, 60 years ago.

The self-styled Queen City of Lafourche Parish, Thibodaux was named for a local plantation owner, Henry Schuyler Thibodaux, a New Yorker who arrived in Louisiana in 1794, when he was given a land grant by the controlling Spanish. He lived through the French occupation, and on through the Louisiana Purchase as well, became a justice of the peace for the newly Americanized territory, and he served on the state senate too, between 1812 and 1824. That's when he was made acting governor of the whole of Louisiana, following the resignation (to become a federal judge) of Thomas B. Robertson.

It was only a short tenure — until Henry Johnson was elected — but in 1827 Thibodaux ran again for the office. He died on the campaign trail, on October 24, near Bayou Terrebonne. Three years later, the town of Thibodauxville was incorporated in his honor on the banks of the Bayou Lafourche.

So it's been around a good few years, although the first time I remember ever reading its name was in the pages of the British rock paper *New Musical Express*. Writer Charles Shaar Murray made the

Jayne Mansfield Dies In Auto Smashup

Jerusalem Becomes Single City

Announcing the end of a legend.

necessary hike in 1973, to cover a Dr. Hook and the Medicine Band show at the local Thibodaux Center.

His mind was clearly not on his job.

"The local black radio station pumps out Wilson Pickett, the Jackson Five, Aretha. We pass over the Huey P. Long Bridge, complete with painters . . . we pass endless roadside cafes, each claiming to be the 'Original Creole Gumbo Kitchen.' We brave the speed traps outside the small towns, and brother, lemme tell ya, they are no fun at all."

Murray's party drove through flooded pasture land, and passed the spot where actress Jayne Mansfield was killed in a late-night car smash in June 1967, winding down the Old Spanish Trail that is Route 90, close by the Rigolets, the waterway that travels from Lake Pontchartrain to the gulf. She was on her way from New Orleans to Biloxi, but the air was thick with mosquito repellent that night and a thick white fog that wiped out visibility; when the tractor trailer rig ahead of them slowed to a crawl as the invisibility loomed, Mansfield just kept on going. The impact, said the *St. Petersburg Times* the following day, "peeled back the top of the sedan and Miss Mansfield was decapitated." Even worse, it was two or three days before her head was found, and the law was locked in a race against time to retrieve it. What a souvenir that would have made for the rubber-neckers who flocked to the crash sight the morning after the accident.

"What else?" mused Murray. "Eventually, here it is. Thibodaux, Louisiana. Population: 15,396. It's not even a one-horse town. They probably have to borrow the horse from the next town along, and it's the kind of place where the sheriff from Redneck Creek, Georgia, takes his best friend's 15-year-old daughter Cindy Lou for dirty weekends.

"One hotel, right? And un-made roads to boot."

Yeah, it's changed a lot since then, although you still can't shake the sensation that the past four decades have just veneered what's really lurking underneath, and if you peel back a corner, the past will reach out and pull you in. And, if you're lucky, it may just feed you.

The father of modern country music, Hank Williams, wrote "Jambalaya" around 1951, although he based his effort on another song entirely, a traditional Cajun number that bemoaned the tragic tale of losing your woman to a man from "Grand Texas." That song is now as good as lost, at least so far as the world at large is concerned. But, in creating a lyric of his own, Williams saw his new song thoroughly reabsorbed into the musical framework from which it was originally carjacked. Today, there are people who believe that "Jambalaya" is as authentic as . . . well, as authentic as jambalaya. And there are others who don't believe that Williams wrote a word of it.

Instead, he purchased it outright from an unknown songsmith — a fairly common practice in the decades before music became an industry. Or maybe he bought it from the great Moon Mullican, a Texan country singer whom Williams once described as his own all-time favorite singer, which is the saga that a lot of people now adhere to. In this version of the story, Mullican was spending time at a small bar located just south of the Choupique Bayou, where Yvonne, whom "kinfolk come to see . . . by the dozen," was the bar's owner — a woman named Yvonne Little. Mullican had a great time there, and had some great food, and when he got home he wrote a song about his evening. Simple.

Williams' supporters, on the other hand, date "Jambalaya" to the singer's time with the *Louisiana Hayride*, overlooking the fact that Shreveport, home of the *Hayride*, is about as far from Cajun culture as it is possible to get without physically upping and leaving the state

— which is not to say, of course, that he could not have sampled the three Cajun dishes that comprise the song's chorus, and it might even go some way towards explaining, or at least excusing, the subschoolboy French into which the lyric lapses on occasion.

These same supporters also point to Williams' hand in a sequel to "Jambalaya," the likeminded "I'm Yvonne (of the Bayou)," which he allegedly composed with Jimmy Rule. Or maybe Moon Mullican wrote that one as well. Ah, rumor and gossip, where would we be without them?

Williams' "Jambalaya" topped the U.S. country chart for a staggering 14 weeks in 1952; near simultaneously, another country singer, Jo Stafford, saw her swiftly recorded spoiler version reach number three on the pop chart. Since that time, Jerry Lee Lewis, Brenda Lee, Fats Domino, Emmylou Harris, John Fogerty and a few hundred more have all lined up to record their own interpretations of what is truly one of Williams' most pervasive ditties. Its magic isn't confined to the United States, either. Indian singer Usher Iyer's 1968 version went on to become one of the biggest-selling English-language records in subcontinental history, while the Carpenters scored a massive hit with the song in the United Kingdom in the early 1970s, and deservedly so.

A lot of people claim to hate their version; even fans of the Carpenters have been known to recoil at it. But Richard lays out a sparkling arrangement, and Karen not only comes across as sweet and sexy, as her best performances insist she was, she actually sounds like she's enjoying herself too — not like some of the sourpusses who have squawked through the song, as though they're reading out their shopping list to a roomful of sawhorses. True, the accompanying flute is an indisputably annoying addition to the party. But, when Karen warns you sons of a gun that we're gonna have big fun on the bayou, you know she means it. Even Hank didn't seem too sure about that.

Jambalaya

1/2 pound cubed boneless chicken

1/2 pound shrimp, boiled and peeled

1 pound hot smoked sausage, andouille or chaurice, sliced

1 large onion, chopped

1 bell pepper, chopped

4 cloves garlic, minced

4 stalks celery, including leaves, chopped

1 small can tomato paste

4 large tomatoes with juice, peeled, seeded and diced

8 cups dark chicken stock

2 teaspoons cayenne

2 teaspoons black pepper

1 teaspoon white pepper

1 teaspoon oregano

1/2 teaspoon thyme

2 bay leaves

salt to taste

4 cups long-grain white rice, uncooked

In a sauté or frying pan, brown the chicken, season with salt, black pepper and white pepper. Remove.

Brown then remove sliced smoked sausage or andouille and pour off some of the fat.

Add the onions, garlic, peppers and celery in oil until onions begin to turn transparent. Add the tomato paste, stir well and simmer till the vegetables are tender-crisp. Deglaze the pan with two cups of stock, scraping the bottom of the pan to mix up any browned remnants. Stir until smooth, and the sautéed vegetables, paste and stock are combined thoroughly.

Add the seasoning, tomatoes and salt to taste. Cook over low-medium heat for about 10 minutes. Add the meat and seafood and cook another 10 minutes. Add the rest of the stock and seasonings, and stir in the rice, combining thoroughly. Cook for about 20–25 minutes, or until the rice has absorbed all the liquid and is cooked through.

Crawfish Pie

1 medium to large onion
3 stalks of celery
6 cloves of garlic
1 can of cream of mushroom soup
1 can light or regular evaporated milk
1 pound of crawfish tails
5 tablespoons of cornstarch
pie crust for 2-crust pie

Preheat oven to 350 degrees. Sauté onions, celery and garlic in butter or olive oil. Add milk and soup and bring to a medium boil. Add crawfish. Maintain medium boil and then add corn starch. Lower heat and cook for another 10 minutes or until thick. Grease pie shell with butter and place in bottom of pan; then add thickened mixture. Put on top shell and bake at 350 degrees for 20 minutes.

Filé Gumbo

1 chicken

knuckle of veal

1 onion

1 quart oysters

salt, cayenne pepper, white pepper

powdered filé

Cut up the chicken and fry in pan with the sliced onion. Place knuckle of veal in a soup pot covered in 3½ quarts of cold water. Add the chicken and allow to simmer about six hours. Strain soup and skim off all fat. Add oysters, cayenne pepper, white pepper. When boiling, sprinkle in, or sift in, powdered filé enough to thicken it.

Then again, it's not as if Thibodaux doesn't have a history to match its musical record, a big bad moon that rises over a catalog of gory death and dismemberment, unrest and outrage that culminates with the memory of the Thibodaux Massacre of November 1887.

Enshrined in the annals as one of the bloodiest labor disputes in U.S. history, at the same time most historians agree that the Thibodaux Massacre is one of the most obscure events in Louisiana's storied past. The Thibodaux Massacre was sparked when the Louisiana Sugar Producers' Association (the LSPA) rejected a demand by local workers to begin paying them in federal cash, rather than company scrip. The average cane picker was taking home around $13 per month at that time (approximately $300 in modern terms), but it could be redeemed only in the LSPA's own stores, at prices that the company itself set. As one can probably imagine, these were considerably higher than those of any other merchant in town.

Greetings from Thibodaux!

Encouraged by the Knights of Labor union, which had just moved into the area with the organization of workers on the Charles Morgan Railroad and Paddle Steamer Company, the newly formed Local Assembly 8404 presented their demands to the LSPA in October 1887. The answer came back a few days later, a resounding no, and on November 1, at the height of the crucial harvest period known as "grinding," 10,000 workers, 90 percent of them African-American, launched a strike across sugar plantations in St. Mary, Lafourche and Terrebonne Parishes.

The company hit back by demanding that the strikers vacate the company-owned cabins in which they lived, and, when those demands were refused, local sheriffs were sent in to evict them. They were unsuccessful.

The plantation owners' rage was fuelled by the knowledge that a major freeze was on its way. If the strike was not resolved within days, the entire crop might be lost. However, help was at hand for the plantation owners. The state governor, Samuel Douglas McEnery, was himself a plantation owner and, as soon as word of the dispute reached him, together with an entreaty from his LSPA contemporaries, he ordered in the state militia. As for the presence of white workers within the striking masses, he could barely contain his contempt. "God Almighty has himself drawn the color line," he declared. Any man who dared cross it presumably deserved whatever fate he received.

On November 1, 1887, the first two companies of militia arrived in nearby Schriever from New Orleans and then headed up to Thibodaux, to store their equipment in front of the antebellum Greek Revival building that served (and still serves) as the Lafourche Parish courthouse. The equipment included horses, provisions, Springfield rifles and, ominously, a Gatling gun, a rapid-fire predecessor of the machine gun that the manufacturers insisted could fire up to 1,200 rounds per minute. It couldn't, but the advertizing spiel must have been amazing.

At first the troops merely contented themselves with assisting with the evictions, and protecting the scab laborers who had been called in to replace the strikers. It seemed to be working, too. Faced with so much obvious firepower, the majority of the strikers abandoned the plantations and headed into Thibodaux, congregating in the African-American ghetto area while they planned their next move. And everybody waited for it.

The stalemate dragged on, first for days, then for weeks. It is unlikely that even the strikers knew what they intended to do next. Elsewhere around Thibodaux, however, fearful white residents had their own opinions. A rumor began to circulate that the strikers intended to torch the entire city. At the same time, word came down from Terrebonne Parish that the first gunshots had been heard, militant pickets firing upon white strikebreakers, and from Lafourche Parish, where guns were being fired into the sugar mills, again by the strikers.

White vigilantes began to take up position around Thibodaux,

Main Street looking East, Thibodaux, La.

Downtown Thibodaux a century ago.

ostensibly as fire watchers, but also as an unofficial police force. It was when two of these vigilantes were shot and injured on the edge of the ghetto that an uneasy truce burst into all-out warfare. On November 23, mounted vigilantes stormed the area, firing indiscriminately, putting buildings to the torch, and beating anybody who crossed their path.

What amounted to an all-white lynch mob rounded up strikers and their family members alike on the spot where present-day Canal Boulevard (which was a canal back then) meets Bayou Lafourche; the blacks were told to run for their lives. They were then cut down, not only by the armed townspeople, but also by the state militia. Precise casualty figures have never been calculated, but it is generally believed that up to 35 black strikers were slaughtered that morning, and some estimates soar 10 times as high.

Other sources, however, erred on the side of caution, particularly in the pages of the white press of the day. "Six killed and five wounded" was a common report. A black paper, however, insisted: "From an eye witness to the whole transaction, we learn that no less than 35 Negroes were killed outright. Lame men and blind women shot; children and hoary-headed grandsires ruthlessly swept down! The Negroes offered no resistance; they could not, as the killing was unexpected."

The strike ended that day, and the workers returned to the fields. They continued to be paid in LSPA scrip.

The massacre is all but forgotten today, but memories were not so short at the time, and, three years later, a grisly postscript came close to being delivered. On August 31, 1890, a party of firefighters from New Iberia took an excursion by railroad into Thibodaux, accompanied by the local African-American string band, whose leader, Joe Adams, happened to have been one of the men run out of Thibodaux on pain of death in the aftermath of the strike.

As soon as word reached Thibodaux of Adams' return, plans were made to murder him — not only for past "crimes," but also because the city had strict laws against blacks enjoying any kind of privileges, including the right to play music. Adams was assaulted on the train, and almost pushed off the moving carriage; he was then shot at three times, while two white men who attempted to go to his aid, New Iberia City Marshall Mr. Pattin and a Thibodaux resident, Mr. Riggins, were also injured. For the second time in three years, Adams survived the wrath of the local townspeople, but the ghosts of those less fortunate surely linger around Canal Street, just as the victims of the city's other crimes and killings might well still stalk the scenes of their deaths.

As is so often, frustratingly, the case, many of these ghosts exist in a ghostly neverwhere of their own, caught in that cultural no-man's-land that exists between hard fact and local legend, one that is mapped out only by scant and scarcely informative sentences that you chance upon in books and on websites that catalog a neighborhood's so-called spooks. No world-renowned specters, these; no headless horsemen of Sleepy Hollow, or Anne Boleyn prowling with her head beneath her arm. These are the ghosts that probably don't even believe in themselves. Some of them have been seen by several people, others by just one or two. Some may even be figments of a single imagination.

But the act of repeating these tales gives them a certain verisimilitude, and it really doesn't matter that we have no concrete circumstance to back them up, that we cannot tie their hauntings to any specific incidents or murders. The tourists still shiver at the prospect of encountering the tightly bound woman who's been seen drinking diesel from a pump, tremble at the thought of meeting the man with half a head who walks a spectral German shepherd, the bloody bride espied beside a corpse in Acadia Park or the woman with a spear through her head who has been sighted in a local store.

There's the half-man, half-horse creature that reputedly dwells in the Onion Bayou, way to the north of the city; there's the mud-drenched corpse with a machete in his head, seen hauling itself out of Devil Swamp and demanding that passersby help solve his grisly murder.

For a moment, you wonder what his story might be, what he might be wearing beneath that coating of swamp slime? An old-time sheriff's uniform, perhaps, his star rusted and crusty, his revolver clogged and useless. . . .

It was time to hunt down Amos Moses.

TRACK SIX

"Amos Moses" by the Sensational Alex Harvey Band
from the LP *SAHB Stories* (Mountain Records)
1976

"Fuck me, I'm lost," I said (though I knew she was sleeping).

The CD, a collection of Jerry Reed's greatest hits, answered back immediately. "Sure can get lost in the Louisiana bayou . . . ," and, about 45 minutes southeast of Thibodaux, we drew to a halt, and pondered the last words a toothless old storyteller named Tom had said to us earlier that same day: "Amos Moses, you said?"

Tom had stared into space for a few minutes, and we thought we'd lost him completely. He did that a lot, just paused in the middle of an accented sentence, and then kept the pause going for so long that it felt like he might never speak again. Too many memories crowding in on his thoughts, too many images on the edge of remembrance. I lit a cigarette to match the ones he was enthusiastically chain-smoking, and while I waited, he dredged through my past.

A past where folk like Amos Moses were as familiar as the hairs on your palm.

Tom finally spoke. "Amos Moses? No, I can't say I know him. But if it's 'gator hunting you're interested in, I might just know a fellow who can help you."

We shook our heads and took our leave. We had a long way to go before nightfall.

Amos Moses, says the song, was a Cajun, the son of Doc Milsap and his pretty wife Hanna, and if you dig into the old Louisiana state documents, there *was* a Mose Milsap whose birth was registered in an undetermined part of the state in 1884.

More than that, though, the historical record keeps silent, and so it should — when I spoke with him in the mid-1990s, the song's composer, Jerry Reed, laughed at the suggestion that Amos Moses was anything more than a figment of his imagination. Maybe he had heard something long ago that set his mind running in that direction, but it was just as likely that he hadn't. Reed told me, "so you just go look for him anyway. If he didn't exist, then there's still plenty like him."

Jerry Reed Hubbard was born in Atlanta, Georgia, on March 20, 1937, but spent the first seven years of his life in and out of foster homes and orphanages after his parents split up just four months after his birth. He was reunited with his mother and her second husband in 1944.

Even as a child, it is said, he was convinced he was going to become a musician; more than that, he was going to be a star in Nashville. He learned to play guitar at age eight, when his mother bought him a two-dollar instrument and showed him how to play a G-chord. Eight years later, he dropped out of high school to tour with Faron Young and Ernest Tubb, and, in 1955, he was discovered by producer Bill Lowery and cut his first single, "If the Good Lord's Willing and the Creek Don't Rise." He signed with Capitol Records and inched along gently until 1958, when label mate Gene Vincent covered one of Reed's songs, the hyper-infectious "Crazy Legs." Reed's own first country hit, "Soldier's Joy," followed in 1959 — ironically around the same time as Reed himself was called up by the military.

Returning to civilian life in 1961, Reed moved to Nashville to find himself already in demand, after Brenda Lee covered his "That's All

You Gotta Do." He was soon scoring minor hits of his own: a cover of Lead Belly's "Goodnight Irene" made number 79; his own "Hully Gully Guitar" reached number 99. He toured with whoever asked him and played guitar on a string of sessions. And, though his recording career rumbled on, it was way below most people's radar. Most people's, but not Elvis Presley's.

Reed was fishing on the Cumberland River the day he received the call. Felton Jarvis, Presley's producer at the time, phoned Reed to ask how he got the distinctive guitar sound on his latest single, "Guitar Man"; Presley and his band had been trying to nail it all day, but Elvis was adamant that he wanted Reed's sound. "Well," replied Reed, "if you want it to sound like that, you're going to have to get me in there to play it."

Reed's version of "Guitar Man" was already eating up the country charts when Elvis covered it; Presley, however, would take it into the pop world, and Reed knew it. He made his way to the studio, and the moment he hit that intro, Presley's face lit up like the Fourth of July. "Then after he got through that, he cut [my] 'U.S. Male' at the same session. I was toppin' cotton, son."

Reed also played the guitar on "Too Much Monkey Business," recorded during that same burst of frenetic creativity, and then launched his own pop chart career with a new song written *about* Presley, "Tupelo Mississippi Flash." But it was "Amos Moses" who confirmed Reed's arrival.

Reed's first genuine crossover hit — a record that blended country and rock, and then added a dash of Cajun into the mix — was originally intended for nothing more glamorous than a B side. It was recorded during the sessions for Reed's *Georgia Sunshine* album on November 5, 1969, at RCA's Nashville Sound studio, and then sent quietly out on the backside of his "The Preacher and the Bear" country hit early in the new year.

"And then some DJs started playing the flip," Reed recalled, "and we started to see some action on the rock stations, so we turned the single over." That Halloween, "Amos Moses" made its bow on the Hot 100. It ultimately reached number eight, and stayed on the chart for an astonishing six months — a success, he insisted, that was the result of an oath he swore to himself after the Elvis Presley experience.

Reed told writer Geoff Lane, "I made myself a promise . . . [that] I was just going to record what I felt — wasn't going to question it, label it, or worry about it. First thing you know, wham, I got a hit. Never had a hit in my life. So I think I'm right now, and I'm gonna stay right where I am.

"People [. . .] have a tendency to say you're country because you come from Nashville. I don't think I'm country country. I was raised in the country and grew up on country music. But I don't make country music. When you say 'country music' to people here, they think of fiddles, steels and three chords. People want to put tags on you [. . . ;] when I first went to L.A. they thought I was colored 'til they saw me."

And the first time Reed went to Louisiana, "it was [so] hot [that] after 48 hours, all the hair in my nose began to mildew. I've loved that place ever since."

It was there and then that he wrote "Amos Moses," building the song around a simple bayou murder mystery. Amos hunted 'gators; the local sheriff hunted Amos. But only one of them would ever come out of the swamp alive.

Leaving Thibodaux on the Old Schriever Highway, civilization sprawls in every direction, and it's only late at night that the darkness truly closes in on you, and offers even a suggestion of the land that Amos Moses knew so well.

Back then, the road started narrowing even before you left the city limits, two lanes down to one, and ultimately down to something a few rungs up from a rutted pathway, your tires trapped in the grooves left by countless beat-up pickups as they wound their way back and forth. Now it was all blacktop and white lines, speed limits and more traffic cops than any highway could need. Seems the youngsters have taken to piling down here at night, driving so fast that you'd need a chopper to catch them, so the police don't even bother with the pursuit. They just wait at either end of the road, one to clock the kids as they pass, and the other to wait for them to appear. The cops can calculate their speed from how long it takes them to make the trip, and the only thing the law needs to watch out for is that the kids see the cruiser in time to hit the brakes.

Forty-five minutes southeast, the song says, but is that for an experienced driver or not? A first timer used to have trouble getting over 25 miles per hour, as the bumps and potholes sent the suspension screaming, and every corner could conceal the speeding death-trap of an oncoming rust bucket. Even today, it can be a precipitous ride, especially when the air gets so thick that you can hear the engine screaming in protest, and so humid that only a fish would leave the windows open. So the AC howls like a banshee, as if desperate to make itself heard above the nightlife, but it's still fighting a losing battle. They say they have bugs here the size of a man's arm, and critters that could chew that arm off.

Past Schriever and the turnoffs to Gray and Houma, we may be able to get a room for the night in Chauvin or Dulac; in fact, we'd be foolish not to, because there really isn't anyplace else down here, and not even the locals would want to spend the night in a car. Some of them wouldn't drive this far for no practical reason, and, not for the first time, we curse the missed connections that saw us setting out later than we'd ever intended.

At the same time, though, Rabbit Bayou at sunset is a beautiful sight, the reds burning through the thick dark green, and you can sense the night shift coming in to work, to chirrup and caterwaul the darkness through; slow down, or even stop the car, and you know that yellow eyes would light up all around you, but we resist the temptation. Who knows if we'd ever be able to start up again?

With the night, the air is getting thicker now. Shadows that we'd once have passed without a second glance loom out as ever more

CAPTURING AN INHABITANT OF THE MARSHES NEAR LAKE PONTCHARTRAIN, LA.

It's tiny enough to be cute, but the jaws could still take off your hand.

menacing spectacles. Somewhere on this highway, or one like it (such tales are rarely as specific as you'd like), we've heard that passing motorists run a gauntlet of ghostly spittle, hawked out by the specter of a woman who has worms squirming out of her mouth — nobody seems to know who she was, or why she has such an unhygienic haunt. I learned one thing that night, as the windshield wipers clicked and clogged across the corpses: it's amazing that anybody even notices her handiwork, through the thick film of squashed bug life that is already caked across the windshield.

Maybe we should have stayed in Thibodaux after all.

Back to "Amos Moses."

If you don't know the song (although it's hard to believe that you don't), Jerry Reed's original version is the acknowledged classic. A live rearrangement, recorded shortly before his death, is the most dramatic updating. But the most powerfully evocative take of them all was recorded in 1976 by the Scottish rock band, the Sensational Alex Harvey Band, for inclusion on their latest LP *SAHB Stories*.

SAHB had been around since the beginning of the decade, the marriage between the 35-year-old Alex Harvey, a longtime fixture on the British scene, and a young band called Teargas. Famed for their extravagantly theatrical shows, and Harvey's genius for onstage characterization, the band spent five years searching for their breakthrough hit; it arrived in 1975, in the form of an in-concert cover of Tom Jones' murder ballad "Delilah."

The self-composed "Boston Tea Party" followed it into the British charts the following year; what the *New Musical Express* called "a nagging, snarling 'Smokestack Lightnin'-style reading of Jerry Reed's sublime 'Amos Moses'" was the follow-up to that.

It's a slow burner, for sure. It fades in gently, that saw-toothed guitar line chasing its tail, a single bass thump like a far-distant thunderclap, and Harvey himself sounding distant, uncertain. But he gets through the first verse, and then something happens; the band comes in with the force of a jaw snap, and everything coils out from there, Harvey's voice rising and the band rising up to meet him. And when Harvey prefaces the instrumental break by announcing, "Here comes Amos," you can hear the man, see the man, striding through the swamp, a 'gator by the tail in one hand, his stump batting insects out of his eyes, a music video for the mind before MTV was ever even dreamed of.

It should have been enormous, should have been the record that sent the Sensational Alex Harvey Band soaring to the top of the tree. But it wasn't, and, when the band broke up a year or so later, it really didn't feel like anyone even noticed.

But they're playing on the CD as we finally pull up into a motel parking lot, and they'll be playing in our heads as we look for some place to eat.

Eating with Amos — Alligator Recipes

Alligator Balls

1 pound chopped alligator meat
1 tablespoon finely chopped onion
2 tablespoons finely chopped celery
1 tablespoon finely chopped parsley
2 tablespoons finely chopped shallots
2 tablespoons lemon pepper
1/2 tablespoon salt
1/2 cup breadcrumbs
1 cup cooking oil
flour to dredge

Combine all ingredients, then form them into one-inch balls. Set aside for an hour until firm, then dredge with flour and fry until brown.

Baked Alligator

6 alligator fillets
lemon juice
lemon slices
garlic powder
butter
chopped parsley
salt and pepper to taste

Arrange alligator fillets in a single layer in a large ovenware dish and sprinkle with salt, pepper and garlic. Squeeze the lemon juice over fillets, then place generous squares of butter over the fillets. Arrange the lemon slices over the fillets and sprinkle with parsley. Bake at 375 degrees until fillets are cooked through.

Grilled Gator

2 pounds alligator fillets
1 tablespoon onion powder
1 tablespoon garlic salt
1 tablespoon butter for each fillet

Season fillets with onion and garlic, dot with butter, then wrap and seal in aluminum foil and place on medium grill for 20 minutes. Flip halfway through cooking.

Gator Burgers

5 pounds ground alligator meat
2 onions minced
3 potatoes diced small
3 bread slices diced small

Season with salt, pepper and garlic powder. Mix the ingredients and form into patties. Pan fry until golden brown.

Alligator Broulettes

2 pounds alligator
2 egg yolks
1/2 bell pepper
oil for frying
2 stalks celery
salt and pepper to taste
milk
3 slices of bread
2 onions
1 cup water

Grind the alligator, onions, celery and bell pepper together. Soak the bread in milk and press out, then add to the ground mixture. Add egg yolks and season to taste. Spoon into hot oil and brown. Remove and place in a pot of boiling water, cover and steam on low heat for 35 minutes.

Beer Fried Alligator

1 pound alligator meat
flour

Trim meat and cut into finger-sized pieces, to be soaked in beer overnight. Drain. Deep fat fry until golden brown.

Alligator Spaghetti

3 pounds alligator meat
3 6-ounce cans of tomato paste
4 teaspoons salt
1 cup minced bell pepper
1/2 cup chopped parsley
2 cups minced onion
1/2 cup Worcestershire sauce
1 pound mushroom stems and pieces
3 cans (2 pounds, 3 ounces each) tomatoes
4 teaspoons oregano
3 cloves minced garlic
3 tablespoons sweet basil
1/2 pound sliced bacon, diced
1 1/2 cups water
1/2 teaspoon Tabasco

Fry the bacon until crisp. Remove the bacon and most of the fat, leaving approximately 4 tablespoons. Cut alligator meat into 1-inch cubes and brown, then set aside. Sauté onions, drained mushrooms, bell pepper and garlic for 10 minutes. Stir in the remainder of the ingredients. Bring to a boil; reduce heat and simmer, uncovered, stirring occasionally, for 3 hours or longer. Now add the alligator meat and simmer until tender. Serve over spaghetti with Parmesan cheese.

Alligator and Scallops

4 alligator steaks — 1 inch thick

1 egg

1 cup milk

1/2 cup butter

Trim all fat from steaks, then cut and pound steaks until 1-inch thick. Beat egg and add milk. Dip each steak into egg mixture. Heat butter and sauté steaks on each side 2 to 4 minutes.

Soup du Crocodile

2 pounds alligator meat, cubed

2 tablespoons oil

1 cup roux

1 cup onion, chopped

1 cup celery, chopped

2/3 cup bell pepper, chopped

1 pound can whole tomatoes in juice

1 lemon sliced across

1 tablespoon salt

1 teaspoon garlic powder

1 teaspoon black pepper

> 2-inch cut basil sprigs
> 2 quarts water
> 4 tablespoons parsley
>
> Heat oil. Add meat, onion, celery, bell peppers, roux, lemon, tomatoes and juice, seasonings and herbs. Stir well while adding water and bring to a boil. Cover and simmer 2½ hours or until meat is tender. Add parsley and simmer a few minutes more.

Amos grew up hunting alligator, or *cocodrie* as the Cajun call 'em. His pa, Doc Milsap, saw to that. As a boy, Amos grew accustomed to baiting his father's hook; in fact, he was the hook. And the bait. With a rope tied around his waist, he would wait in the water until a 'gator caught sight of him. As it lunged, his father would tug the rope, hauling Amos from the water and then blasting the alligator in much the same movement.

Now, there's a lot of bayou boys who grew up with a rope around their waist, scampering around their father's crab- or shrimp-fishing boat, with the other end hooked to a winch. In their cases, though, the rope was intended to prevent them from falling into the water, at least until they gained their river legs and could be trusted to move around without the harness. Or else they'd dangle over the side, to free the nets from some kind of underwater obstruction. After so many thousands of years of regular flooding, you can find anything beneath the bayou waters, including the vast, intractable pipelines that run from the oil and gas fields that pock, pollute and (just as damaging) dredge the bayou, as well as sundry relics of past floods — everything from submerged motor cars to ruined homesteads. The "uncharted wrecks of wonder" with which punk songwriter TV Smith littered the song "Drowning Men" take on a whole new meaning here.

Most of all, though, it'll be old tree trunks, drowned mangrove and cypress for the most part, and many a vessel has come to grief, or at least lost its nets, to a gnarly old stump clinging to the trailing net like a drowning man clutching at a rope. It can take hours of patient, cautious negotiation to free the nets from their grasp, inching the boat back and forth above the snarl, hoping it will untangle itself, and a pair of small hands working in the water as well might make the difference between a wasted afternoon and an entire night trying to free yourself. Only as a last ditch effort would you cut the nets free, not because they're expensive in themselves, but because any expense at all cuts into the profits of a fishing trip, and with fuel having already accounted for a large chunk of them, anything else should be avoided at all costs.

Almost all, anyway. A boat only needs to be stationary (or there-abouts) for a few minutes before the first reptilian eyeballs will focus on it, and the darker it gets, the more eyes there will be. Alligators are not the omnipresent threat they used to be, too, at least in Louisiana; Florida suffers far greater damage from the critters, but even there the average tops out at no more than seven unprovoked attacks on humans per year. Published statistics add the further assurance that just one in 28 of these will be fatal. So that's alright, then.

It's an urban myth that a 'gator will disable a man first by swishing its tail and breaking his legs, before moving in for the kill. Why would they need to? Moving far faster than any creature that size should be able to, a 'gator simply latches its jaws onto the nearest appendage, sinks in its razor-sharp, cone-shaped teeth, and then spins its body until the limb is literally twisted and ripped away.

Most human victims, however, never experience that. One bite informs the 'gator that its prey maybe isn't what it thought, and the beast will leave nothing more than puncture wounds — which themselves are nothing to laugh about, but at least the limb is still in place. Far tastier to the average alligator are cattle, waterfowl, wildlife, domestic dogs and cats (should human homesteads get too close to their habitat) and even other alligators. Man is fairly low on the average alligator's menu, which means Amos was probably just unlucky the day that he got bit, although that's another part of the song's mystique, the fact that Amos only has one arm. Or one and a half, if you want to be picky about it.

The Ten Activities Most Likely to Precipitate an Alligator Attack

1. Attempting to capture or pick up an alligator
2. Swimming
3. Fishing or fishing-related activities
4. Retrieving golf balls
5. Walking in water
6. Snorkeling
7. Disturbing/clearing weeds and plant life on riverbank
8. Standing/sitting on riverbank
9. Falling from a boat
10. Canoeing

There he was, sitting in the swamp with the rope around his waist, and maybe Doc was simply a little too slow hauling him back onto the boat, or perhaps the 'gator was a little too fast. Either way, it had Amos' left forearm off in a second, all the way up to the elbow. Bayou fishermen see such injuries a lot, although it's the winches on their boats, rather than the wildlife in the water, that accounts for most of the mutilations. And every single victim does more or less what Amos was forced to do: wait for the wound to heal and then replace it with some kind of prosthetic. They usually return to work as well, and that's exactly what Amos did. Only now he had a new weapon to use against the marauding reptiles. He would knock them cold with a bang on the head from his stump.

A storm in the bayou, from a 19th-century illustration that appeared in Frank Lesley's Illustrated Newspaper *in 1886.*

It's not a method most hunters would recommend, although, from the time-honored hook and line through to the razor-sharp barbed arrows fired from a modern compound bow, there are probably as many different ways of hunting 'gator as there are hunters.

Alligator hunting has been legal in Louisiana only since 1987; for 20 years before that, since 1967, it was strictly prohibited, as wildlife officials struggled to pull the American alligator (*Alligator mississippiensis*) off the endangered species list. A creature whose range once reached from the Carolinas to Texas, and as far north as Arkansas, was staring extinction in the face.

Of course, that did not halt the trade in alligator skin — a trade that Amos Moses had pursued since he was young enough to float, and which his daddy had followed before him. Every night, a man who grew up devouring his weight in groceries, and who needed just one hand to kill a monster reptile, would be out in the bayou, waiting for his prey. Except one night, it was Amos who was being hunted, by a local sheriff who was determined to uphold the law and save the 'gators.

Nobody ever saw him again.

"I don't know what happened to the sheriff," Reed laughed. "I just wrote the song. He went in to wait for Amos, and he never came out again. Maybe he got lost, maybe he got eaten. . . . Or maybe he's lying in the mud with a machete in his skull, emerging at night, dripping in gloop, to howl for passersby to bring him justice.

TRACK SEVEN

"I Walk on Gilded Splinters" by Dr. John
from the LP *Gris-Gris* (Atco)
1969

The land of Los Isleños lies southeast of New Orleans, a corner of Saint Bernard Parish that owes its genesis to the Canary Islanders who settled here in one great wave between 1778 and 1783, and who were still speaking their own, uniquely rustic brand of Castillian into the early 20th century. The settlement itself was originally called La Concepción and, a little later, Nueva Gálvez. When the French displaced the Spanish, it was renamed Terre aux Boeufs — the land of cattle.

By the early 1790s, however, the region's Spanish governor, Bernardo de Gálvez, had given his name to the region — although many visitors to the area overlook the relics of Gálvez's reign entirely, and fix on Saint Bernard Parish's other historical claim to fame. It was here, on January 8, 1815, that the Battle of New Orleans was fought, the final combat of the War of 1812 — and the fact that the war itself had ended two weeks earlier, without either the defending Americans or the attacking English being aware of the fact, merely adds piquancy to what is still regarded as America's greatest land victory ever. Or else it reminds us how much fun we used to have, before the invention of the telephone.

It was here, too, that one of New Orleans' most beloved musical sons, Mac "Dr. John" Rebennack, came face to face not with a vengeful ghost from Saint Bernard's past, but with the equally irate spirit of its present, the voodoo priestess Queen Julia Jackson. She was stately and stentorian in a riot of costuming that Dr. John originally mistook for a long-mothballed Mardi Gras outfit before he realized these were the lady's daily clothes; she swept backstage without an ounce of ceremony.

"Dr. John, I got to talk to you. Do you know who I am?"

He didn't, so she told him. "I'm Queen Julia Jackson, and what you said about me in your song was a goddamned lie."

A goddamned lie. Three years before, in 1969, Dr. John released his debut LP, the mystic potpourri of *Gris-Gris.* And there, buried within its manifold folds, there lurked a single song of such pristine pop prettiness that it was impossible not to pay attention to it. It was called "Jump Sturdy" — not a command or an invitation, not Texan slang for rabbit, or even a once-popular New Orleans liquor (although that's probably what she was named after), but a beautiful Creole dancing girl, who came "out of the swamp like a crazy fool," who could dance with fish and juggle with fire, and who once conjured up lightning on the Bayou St. John, the same stretch of land where the witch queen Marie Laveau once staged her rituals.

It was in town that Jump met her end, "down on Melpomene and Erato Streets," done to death by the spirit of Zozo Labrique, a 19th-century New Orleans eccentric who, according to Dr. John, was in turn called up by Queen Julia Jackson. And not a word of his tale was true.

Dr. John was playing the "Mardi Gras Mambo" at Leander Perez Hall in Saint Bernard Parish . . . the venue that was named for Leander Henry Perez, the then recently deceased political boss of both the Saint Bernard and Plaquemines Parishes. The parish had a longtime reputation for corruption, and Dr. John was already jumping after a group of undercover narcotics agents appeared back-

Moss-laden "Greetings from Plaquemine," on this WWII-era postcard.

stage, hawking the self-same marijuana they'd just confiscated from the audience. Now here was this old woman stepping straight out of some dark voodoo folktale, accusing him of lying about her.

The Doctor struggled to gain some equilibrium. "I think I im-marble-ized you," he told her, and that was true. For who, outside of her immediate neighborhood, would even have heard of Queen Julia Jackson if it wasn't for the tale of "Jump Sturdy"? But the Queen was having none of it.

"You're never going to be immortal 'til you're dead," she snapped. "Do I look dead to you?" Then she turned and walked away, and he never heard from her again.

As portentous anecdotes go, it's a bit of a wet squib, but it does remind us of one fact. Dr. John brought a lot of names to life, or even back to life, and that included his own.

The Doctor, Mac Rebennack, was a native Louisianan, born in New Orleans in November 1940, and raised in the home that his parents shared with his maternal grandparents, and their personal

The back cover of Dr John's nerve-wracking debut album, Gris-Gris.

repository of local lore and legend.

It was at their knees that young Mac first heard of the Needle Men, medical students from the Charity Hospital, it was said, who stalked the streets in search of fresh bodies to perform their grisly homework on, and not at all careful how they acquired them, either. A needle in a passerby's arm was their favorite method; they'd simply brush hurriedly past you when they met you in the street, and you might not even feel the little prick in your arm, not until you keeled over a few paces later, and the last words that you ever heard would be those of a young man pushing through the gathering crowd: "Let me through, I'm a medical student."

Or some would stick their needle in your eye — or, at least, that's what Grandpa Rebennack told his young grandson. Others hung out at the picture house, jabbing their needles into unwary young women, and then carrying them off to the white slave trade.

Neither were the Needle Men the only medical peril you had to negotiate if you went out walking the city streets at night. There were the Black Bottle Men, who'd offer their hapless victims a drink from, indeed, a black bottle, and then carry their lifeless forms back to Charity. These stories must have made the young boy wonder precisely what kind of hospital it was, one that wasn't content with the usual parade of sick, drunken indigents and pox-bearing whores, but which actually went out soliciting for further business. As benevolent institutions went, Charity Hospital was one whose threshold you never wanted to cross.

Not all of Grandpa's tales were horrific. Some were sad, some were funny, and some were just so damned tragic that their heroes and heroines remained with Mac forever. Zozo Labrique, for instance. True, her name and reputation have been conflated over the years to the status of a voodoo priestess, but who was she really? Nothing much more than a harmless old Creole who walked the streets selling the red brick dust with which the locals scrubbed their stoops and sidewalks. We don't even know her real name — "Zozo" was what the children called her, because she was so small and scrawny that she looked like the zozo bird they'd sung about in playtime; and *la briques* were what she sold. So, Zozo Labrique.

But she would smile and tousle the children's hair when they came close, and if they were lucky she'd hand them a stick of peppermint, bought with the nickels she collected for her wares. And that was the funny thing. She would only accept payment in nickels, which she hoarded in her mattress — and when she was found dead of starvation, with her mattress bulging, the tales of her miserliness spread far and wide. Dr. John just spread her name even further.

By the time he reached his late teens, Rebennack was already steeped in the lore and legend that gave New Orleans its reputation. Now all he needed to do was make that legend his own.

He learned what would become his trade from the Temple of the Innocent Blood, a gathering that he visited for the first time at the end of his teens. There he saw for the first time Sister Caterine, queen of white voodoo; there, too, he met Sister Eunice, from whom he learned both voodoo and the guitar.

She, Sister Eunice, was long dead by the time the Doctor came to talk of her to *Rolling Stone* in 1971, but he continued to think of her in the present tense. It was, he explained to the journalist, the Creole way. "Sister Eunice . . . is an old guitar player who played around New Orleans and in the voodoo church. She don't play too much pop music or anything, but she taught me some jazz tunes and got me interested in some modern jazz numbers. She opened my taste for more kinds of music. We'd sit up all night in the woods and when we'd get through, we'd want to play some more 'cause we were just full of music."

He was filled, too, with voodoo, which he proved when he titled his first album *Gris-Gris*, and then found himself needing to define the term for the world. "The thought behind gris-gris is just like when you send a Hallmark greeting card," he told *Rolling Stone*. "It's the thought behind it. Gris-gris is just like roots and stuff. Like you might wake up and find a cross on your porch with a chicken's foot and some moss wrapped around it. The impression that you get is that you're not welcome or not wanted.

"All voodoo works that way. It's the thought behind it. The thought not only comes from the sender's head, but it goes to the receiver's head. I'll tell you one thing. Gris-gris goes good in bed. [But] it's like anything else, there's a good side and a bad side. [But] you never hear about the good side, because the bad side looks more exciting and better."

Looking for his first musical break, Rebennack haunted Cosimo Matassa's legendary studios, getting to know local musicians and just hanging out. He graduated to playing keyboards and guitar on records by Professor Longhair, Frankie Ford, Joe Tex and others; by 1958, he was established as a songwriter, musician and producer at Johnny Vincent's Ace label, one of the so-called Funk Clique gathering of New Orleans' top session men. The following year, 1959, he released his first single, the ominous "Storm Warning."

In 1964, Rebennack almost lost a finger when he tried to prevent a friend from being pistol-whipped. The injury left him unable to play guitar, so he switched to keyboards, and, around 1965, he relocated to Los Angeles, where he became a regular member of producer Phil Spector's house band.

For a time, Mac kept his magic and his music very separate. True, he might occasionally rewire an old voodoo tune into one of the pop songs he was penning for so many other artists, but there was no conscious attempt to merge the two. It happened, though, as one side of his life began to melt into the other, as his personal tastes became his public persona. Soon, *Rolling Stone* reported happily, his Californian home was "a typical San Fernando Valley tract house, where a human skull voodoo drum shares equal billing with baby bottles and shoes," and a "bizarre and incongruous collection of canes, tape recorders, drums, feathers, records, Zap Comix, drawings of Christ, empty bottles, necklaces, wife and child."

"We had a groove we was into then, riding around [Los Angeles] with candles and incense burning in the car. It wasn't a hippy thing, so much as a mixture of our own New Orleans mystical jive, and the trappings of the old Beat scene."

Rebennack toyed with a couple of groups during this period, the Zu Zu Band (formed with Jessie Hill) and Morgus & the Three Ghouls, both of whom had a lovely line in Halloween horror–type catering. But it was 1967 before he arrived at his future identity, Dr.

John Creaux the Night Tripper, purveyor of dark Creole invocations, secret voodoo ritual, and blistered bayou imagery.

Onstage, outrageous robes and feathered headdresses, scantily clad dancers and liquid lights heightened the impressions left by his lyrics; offstage, his presence alone was enough to immolate the imagination. And, if a witness required any further elucidation, he needed only ask the Doctor about . . . the doctor.

Without Dr. John, we would never have heard of Doctor John. But in New Orleans through the 1840s and 1850s, there was scarcely a soul who hadn't heard of him, and very few who didn't tremble, at least a little, at the mention of his name.

John Montaigne, also known as Bayou John, but better known as Doctor John, was born in what is now Senegal, on the west coast of Africa, sometime around 1800. He may have been a prince; that was his story, anyway. His earthly riches, however, mattered little once he was scooped up by the Spanish slave trade and transported to Cuba, where he was put to work as a cook on one of the island's many plantations — coffee, tobacco or, most likely, sugar.

Somehow he earned his freedom, and he embarked on a career as a seaman, traveling the world, he said, before landing in New Orleans and making it his home. There he found work as a cotton roller at the dockyard, but, more subtly, he established himself as a rootman, or medicine man. His knowledge of herb and plant lore was as extensive as it was awe-inspiring.

Certainly his fellow workers came to fear him, and, so the story goes, John was soon a landowner in his own right, purchasing a property out on Bayou Road, building a home and filling it with female slaves. Later in life, he told of having had over 50 children by his 15 wives — the last of whom, a white woman, supposedly supervised the entire household.

He purchased a carriage and pair, and rode through the city on a blooded saddle horse, garishly costumed in the Spanish style that appealed to his cavalier lifestyle. Only as he approached middle age did he affect a more sobering dress, his tattooed face obscured by a deep black beard, his body shrouded in black and a white frilled shirt. But, if his appearance was eye catching, it was his lifestyle that excited comment and fear. His home was decorated — or, perhaps, alive — with snakes and scorpions, lizards and bugs, and positively festooned with the symbols of Catholicism that his patrons would recognize and be comforted by; voodoo historians frequently describe Doctor John as the first to combine the two traditions into one.

Around a prominently displayed statue of the Virgin Mary, human skulls — which he supposedly had stolen from local grave-yards — decorated every surface. Desiccated toads hung from nails on every wall in the house, while other bones, animal and human, hung as decoration and ornament from ceilings and walls. Every room had its share of them, but mostly they hung in the parlor, where Doctor John entertained his "guests."

Illiterate though he was, Doctor John financed his lifestyle by offering his services as a healer and a fortune teller. He could place and lift curses, offer potions for romance and riches, cure and cause sickness, and all for a fee. Shelves and shelves of bottles concealed elixirs and charms of all descriptions; there was not a request that he could not fulfill with just a few drops of this, a few grains of that and a dash of something else.

At first, his customers were poor blacks, but Doctor John was never going to grow rich from them. He began consorting with the cream of New Orleans society — not necessarily openly, but effec-tively all the same. According to rumor, he had created a vast network of domestic servants placed throughout the city. It was they who passed his name along to their employers should it ever seem that they could use the Doctor's aid and they who then reported back to the Doctor all the little snippets of information that they thought he might be able to employ in his soothsaying. All the household secrets that the "upstairs" folk thought were theirs alone, the quiet peccadilloes and scandals that every home harbored,

Doctor John had them all memorized. Then, when those well-to-dos came to see him, as they inevitably would, how they were startled to learn that simply by looking into their eyes, he had opened a window to their darkest soul.

"One would stand aghást were [one] told the names of the high society dames who were wont to drive to this sooty black Cagliostro's abode, to consult him upon domestic affairs," exclaimed author Henry C. Castellanos; doubtless, one would be even more horrified by the nature of the secrets that Doctor John was able to whisper to them, sexual perversions and financial misdoings, who was cheating and who was lying, and whose entire universe could be shattered with a single misplaced word. Doctor John never resorted to blackmail, it is said, because he did not need to. Simply knowing that another man knew their deepest secrets was sufficient to keep his customers' pocketbooks open. It was widely whispered (for few people dared speak of the Doctor's mysteries aloud) that he had buried over $150,000 worth of money and treasure somewhere in the grounds of his home.

For many years, the Doctor seemed invulnerable, or at least untouchable. Sometime around the 1840s, Doctor John and a woman named Pauline Rebennack were in trouble with the law. (Mac Rebennack never figured out whether or not she was a relative. But how intriguing to imagine that she might have been.) Supposedly they were running a voodoo operation and also, possibly, running a whorehouse. But the law lost interest soon enough.

On other occasions, neighbors would call the authorities in to try to protect themselves from what they believed was the Doctor's supernatural wrath, or at least his malicious mischief making; showers of stones were a common problem in the neighborhood around the Doctor's home, and he made no secret of the fact that he could prevent such disturbances if only the victim was prepared to pay him. On at least one occasion, in 1867, a Mr. Samuel Wilson paid the Doctor $62 to stop a particularly ferocious attack, then sued him for the money's return. The Doctor repaid the sum, and, just days later, the hail of stones returned.

But for all his wisdom, the Doctor was a lousy steward for his riches. On more than one occasion, people he trusted to make investments for him skipped out with his cash, oblivious to any curses that he might subsequently call down upon them. The Doctor moved into retail, opening various small businesses, only to see them fail. Several of his wives and his now adult children departed from his home, usually with however much cash they could carry secreted about their persons. And one day shortly after he taught himself to write — or at least sign his own name — he was persuaded to add his signature to some form of document, only to discover that he had just given away everything he owned. By the end of his life, he was living off the charity of his children, and what a comedown that must have been for him. For the only offspring who would take him in were those of his last wife, the white woman — mulattoes, whom the Doctor had always hated.

Doctor John passed away in late October or early November 1885. His obituary, written by the great New Orleans chronicler Lafcadio Hearn and published in the November 7 edition of *Harper's Weekly*, claimed he was "nearly a hundred years [old]" (in fact, he was closer to 82) and described him as "the most extraordinary African character that ever obtained celebrity within [New Orleans] limits."

Even greater than Marie Laveau, whom Hearn also obituaried, Doctor John bestrode the city like a colossus. Laveau, after all, was "a very wonderful old woman with a very kind heart [and] whatever superstitious stories were written about her, it is at least certain that ... [they] were wholly due to her marvelous skill in the use of native herb medicines, and her ready wit."

Doctor John, on the other hand, might have been, "in many respects, a humbug," Hearn continued. "But he ... believed sincerely in the efficacy of certain superstitious rites of his own. He stated that he had a Master whom he was bound to obey; that he could read the will of his Master in the twinkling of the stars; and often on clear nights, the neighbors used to watch him standing alone at some street corner staring at the welkin [the sky, or more properly, the vault of Heaven], pulling his woolly beard and talking in an unknown language to some imaginary being."

His was a powerful story, but it lingered only a short while. In his own lifetime, the Doctor was clearly eclipsed by the rise of Marie Laveau, and, although most people agreed that she learned much of her magic from the Doctor himself, the pupil clearly had no fear of the teacher. Later, history itself did much to obscure Doctor John's importance to the mid-Victorian city — history, and the efforts, of course, of the rich and successful who had once flooded his coffers with their silver and gold in the hope that he would keep their secrets to himself.

Eighty years after his death, Doctor John was forgotten by everybody bar the occasional voodoo scholar, and students of Lafcadio Hearn himself — five foot three, a one-eyed Greek who spent most of his life being terrified by ghosts. Hearn spent a decade in New Orleans, 1878–1888, and so peopled his period writings and journalism with his impressions of the spectral city that, to his readership, those impressions became reality, sinking so deep into the national subconscious that, long after Hearn was dead and forgotten, his descriptions lingered on.

So, when Doctor John returned from the grave at the end of the 1960s, crackling over FM radio in a sea of rattles, shrieks and incantations, the audience that awaited him might never have ever heard his name, nor imagined such a creature had ever existed. But they *knew* who and what he was, regardless.

Mac Rebennack had been planning the resurrection of Dr. John for a long time, although his initial vision was to send one of his friends, musician Ronnie Barron, out in the role. "But when the time came to cut the songs," Mac recalled, "Ronnie wasn't available. His manager, Don Costa, didn't want him to do it because he wanted to

Private vessels moored on the bayou in St John.

slot Ronnie and his band into a Curtis Mayfield and the Impressions
. . . kind of direction. [So] I decided I would wing it. . . ."

In later years, earnest archaeologists would pinpoint *Gris-Gris*,
his new identity's debut album, as the third key offshoot of the same
psychedelic miasma that spawned the Latin funk of Santana and
Malo and the acid funk of George Clinton and Sly & the Family
Stone. That much could be true, but it's also very misleading. Those
acts drew their sources from within the realms of human experience.
Dr. John's incorporated the un-human as well. "I Walk on Gilded
Splinters," "Danse Kalinda Ba Doom" and "Gris-Gris Gumbo Ya Ya"
dominate, but John's crooked Creole incantations are unforgettable
throughout.

Onstage and off, he stepped out in a suit made of snake, lizard
and alligator skin, hooked together with chamois. "I looked like
Frankenstein coming down the street," he said, and when the outfit
needed repair, he found himself resorting to the taxidermist's trade
for the necessary spare parts. Joined by Jessie Hill — Dr. Poo Pah

Doo — and Dr. (Harold) Battiste of Scorpio, the Night Tripper found other ways of living up to his name, by constructing a dark and freaky ghost train through the kind of bayou backwaters that the tourist guides never visit.

"Smoky and aquatic," said *Rolling Stone*; the sound of "Mose Allison stoned and trapped in a swamp with a chorus of mistaken Baptist harmonies." *Gris-Gris* captivates in every direction. Atlantic Records label head Ahmet Ertegun might once have stared in despair at the record and asked, "How can we market this boogaloo crap?" But anybody who came within a speaker's length of the LP knew that the boogaloo was in the eye of the beholder. Hoodoo haunted *Gris-Gris*, from the moment the needle touched the first groove until long after it departed the final one.

The opening "Gris-Gris Gumbo Ya Ya" sets the stage for all that follows — albeit one that successive years of misinterpretation have seriously skewed. Even the millennial reissue and remaster of *Gris-Gris* boasts liner notes that reckon the song was named, in turn, for the local term for voodoo (Gris-Gris), a regional stew (gumbo) and an old Lee Dorsey hit ("Ya Ya"). One out of three ain't bad, gris-gris is indeed voodoo, but "gumbo ya ya" is a local expression that basically translates as "everyone talks at once," and, as the album meanders through the bayous of Dr. John's imagination, dripping with moisture and heavy with humidity, that is exactly what happens.

There is no respite. Yes, *Gris-Gris* does have its weak moments, most notably the mystifyingly jazz-tinged "Croker Courtbullion." But the remainder of the disc is spellbinding, from the seething atmospherics of "Mama Roux," a song so locked into the regional groove that today there is a Mardi Gras krewe named for it . . . to name your poison and drink it as well. You might never have seen Louisiana in your life, but *Gris-Gris* still showed you around.

Indeed, no matter who else might be regarded as the heart of the Louisiana music scene — and there's a roll call of names if you only care to dig deep enough — its soul would never stray far away from Dr. John's first album and, in particular, from its closing climax, the dripping, decaying sibilance of "I Walk on Gilded Splinters."

Jump Sturdy and Zozo Labrique, Doctor John and Pauline Rebennack — so many images and characters dance through the smoke of *Gris-Gris* that, by the time the first-time listener reaches "I Walk on Gilded Splinters," he must already feel there are no more shocks or surprises to come. Instead, everything the album has already stated is restated in brighter, brittle colors, and, if the lyrics occasionally lurch into incomprehension, then that only exaggerates their importance; no less than the meaning of the album's title, the Internet is alive with misheard renderings of Dr. John's lyrics (including, on one site, the memorable claim that Jump Sturdy was killed with a zozola brick). But the words possess an audible chill regardless.

The backing vocals are Creole curses, the lyrics themselves a brutal invocation, and the music is as intense as it is hypnotic. In the past other artists had touched upon the bayou's sinister underside — Beausoleil's "Zydeco Gris-Gris," for example. But "I Walk on Gilded Splinters" felt like the real thing because, in a lot of ways, it was the real thing. Maybe, if you're really serious about your folklore and religion, it was little more than a B movie, grabbing mass-market superstitions by the scruff of the neck, and sending reality scuttling even further from view. But there's your reality, there's my reality, and there's reality itself, and "I Walk on Gilded Splinters" — all jerking ropes and clouds of smoke, charnal chants and crazy-eye staring — takes a little piece of all three, to create a fourth of its own.

Earning covers from as far afield as soul songstress Marsha Hunt and English rockers Humble Pie, clotheshorse Cher and punk icon Paul Weller, Southern rockers Allman Brothers, indie artists the Flower Pot Men — "Jambalaya" for the rock generation — "I Walk on Gilded Splinters" is the definitive sound of bayou country, the first hiss you hear when you wake up in the morning, the last insectoid rattle before you go to bed at night, the darkness at the height of day, the light that dances in the darkness, the dank, sinister, creeping flesh that a hundred movies and a thousand novelists have tried in vain to recapture as art, invoked instead as timeless ritual.

"I was criticized by some people for my first album because they said I was taking sacred music," the Doc reflected. "They knew nothing about what I was doing. That was no sacred music, that's music I wrote. I patterned it around voodoo church music, but it wasn't exactly the music or the lyrics or nothin'."

It wasn't exactly the music or the lyrics or nothin'. That's what we're talking about here, isn't it? The sound of the bayou isn't any distinguishable individual feature. It's just a feeling, a mood, a set of scales that may peel out of an old pianola, or may have flaked off the back of an alligator.

Moving forward in time, not all of Dr. John's albums were as terrifying as *Gris-Gris*, not all of his songs as powerful as "I Walk on Gilded Splinters" — indeed, by the late 1970s, he had dropped many of the early theatrical stunts and confirmed himself instead as one of America's greatest blues jazzmen. The same psilocybic gumbo nightmare lay at the heart of the best of them, of course, but still "I Walk on Gilded Splinters" stands so high above the rest — so high above many other artists' efforts as well — that it is impossible to resist falling under its spell. Especially when, as Bo Diddley put it in "Who Do You Love," the night was dark although the sky was blue, and the ice truck comes screaming down the alleyway. . . .

TRACK
EIGHT

"Who Do You Love" by Juicy Lucy
from the LP *Juicy Lucy* (Vertigo)
1969

Back to Robert Johnson, or at least *a* Robert Johnson, one of the many who have been enshrined in legend and, in this case, the one that author Stanley Booth immortalized in his play *Standing at the Crossroads*. That was no devil who tuned your geetar, it was just a destitute voodoo man who convinced you to sell him your numb-nuts soul, when all he really wanted to get his hands on was a pair of comfortable shoes. And, once he'd got them, he started walking, down the road, down the years, past milestone after milestone, past wall and fence and hovel, through the swamps and through the plantations, until somewhere around the mid-1950s, he met another Mississippi bluesman, and he helped him to write a song as well, a song about love and redemption and malice. Most of all, malice. The fact that it's the quintessential blues song, quintessential Americana, only adds substance to the story.

Bo Diddley wrote "Who Do You Love" in 1956, one more in that never-ending sucker punch of churning guitar boogies that powered him through the remainder of the decade and essentially laid down the law for every blues band that followed. "Bo Diddley," "I'm a Man," "Diddley Daddy," "Pretty Thing," "Cops and Robbers," "Hey

Bo Diddley," "Mona (I Need You Baby)," "Road Runner" — by the time R & B made it over the ocean and into the heart of a host of British blues bands, Bo Diddley was already arguably past his best, at least so far as his writing went. But his repertoire was a bible, and Bo became a god. A god who wore a cobra snake for a necktie.

Elias "Bo Diddley" Bates was Mississippi born and bred, although there were only a few miles in it. His birthplace, McComb, lies on the fringe of the southern state line, and its namesake, Colonel Henry Simpson McComb, was president of the New Orleans, Jackson and Great Northern Railroad as it carved up the center of Louisiana.

Once headquartered in New Orleans itself, the railroad's staff apparently paid too much heed to the city's bar and leisure scene for the crusty old Colonel's liking. So he upped and transplanted the entire operation to Pike County, Mississippi, 80 miles south of Jackson, 112 miles north of New Orleans. There, three small communities, Elizabethtown, Berglund and Harveytown, were consolidated into one, and just to make sure that his workers behaved themselves, McComb had it written into the city charter that no intoxicating liquors should ever be sold within the limits. If temptation wanted to truant his crew, it would have to come and find them.

Of course it did, and, by the time the man who would be Bo, Elias Bates, was born on December 30, 1928, on a farm just outside town, McComb was as drunken, violent, downtrodden and poverty-stricken as any small city could be. Today it's best known for its railroad museum and its camellias. In fact, modern McComb is known as "The Camellia City of America," and proudly insists that no place in America can boast a larger variety of the heady bloom.

Bo was six when mother Gussie got out of town, following the death of the boy's stepfather, Robert McDaniels; they moved to Chicago, and Diddley never looked back. Except McComb was in his blood, and when he started writing songs, the beat in his head was the beat of the swamps that encircled the city of his youth, echoing through the percussive thwack of the hambone, a relic of

FAMOUS LACE GRILLWORK, NEW ORLEANS, LA. — 217

Some of the country's most beautiful decorative grillwork can still be found around New Orleans.

the days when slaves made prohibited music by slapping their bodies and dancing to the resultant rhythm.

"I worked on this rhythm of mine," Diddley explained. "I'd say it was a mixed-up rhythm, blues and Latin American and some hillbilly, a little spiritual, a little African and a little West Indian calypso. And if I want to start yodeling in the middle of it, I can do that, too. I like gumbo, you dig?"

"Who Do You Love" was gumbo. George R. White, author of Diddley's biography *Bo Diddley: Living Legend*, describes it as "a stunning display of voodooesque braggadocio," and Diddley agreed. "I'm tellin' this chick . . . how bad I am, so she can go tell the cat she's hanging with, 'this dude is something else.' That's what it kinda meant, cat ridin' rattlesnakes and kissin' boa constrictors and stuff." Deadly snakes, headless chickens, all voodoo life is in that lyric if you only care to tear the top off the words, and its narrator himself could be Johnny Blaze, haring out of the carnival sideshow with his head aflame and his heart full of vengeance. Lynyrd Skynyrd lost their lives in the swamps outside of McComb, you know.

Diddley was up in Kansas City when he first heard "Who Do You Love" in his head, listening to a gang of children bigging up to one another, chanting insults at one another, and calling names to a rhythm that intrigued him.

"It was like an African chant, and I wanted words that would suit it." Bluesman Muddy Waters was riding high on the maniacal malice of "I'm Your Hoochie Coochie Man" at the time, a slice of primal braggadocio that portrayed its protagonist as the ultimate tougher-than-tough man. Diddley wanted to "come up with something even rougher."

He succeeded. The opening line came to Bo straightaway, the 47 miles of barbed wire that evoked fenced-in farmland to some ears, penned-in jailbirds to others, but either way was no place you'd want to go for a walk. "But I couldn't get a rhyme for it. I thought of car tires and mule trains, and I couldn't get anything to fit. Then one day I said 'use a cobra snake,' and my drummer, Clifton James, added 'for a necktie.' . . ." And that was it, the song was off and running, a new verse a day until it was done and could be unveiled, ominous, dark and dangerous, seething with unseen evil and simply begging for the chance to sidle into your soul.

Diddley scored a hit, but he was not the only one. You could stuff your stereo with the various versions that have been flung out of Diddley's original drama, and never get tired of the song. The Doors used to build their live show up to it, knowing that in Diddley's lyric every promise that Jim Morrison's still formative poetry had ever made could be justified — even if Morrison usually sounded so out of it by the time they reached the song that the lyrics were all but unintelligible. Still Ray Manzarek washed it in an organ that was as pregnant as it was purposeful, while the drums beat like rain on a rusted tin roof and the guitar swooped in and out around the cypress stumps. Catch the version on the Felt Forum box set; Jim's as out of it as ever, but it's steaming regardless.

Other bands took other stabs, and in 1969 San Francisco's Quicksilver Messenger Service devoted one entire side of their *Happy Trails* album to a marathon live jam through the Diddley rhythm that, you'd assume, would be as far as it could go. You'd be wrong. Quicksilver themselves had only just begun to play with the song, and if you find yourself looking for a definitive retread, hunt down the two-CD retelling of their July 1977 performance at the Quarter Note Lounge in New Orleans. The sound quality's scratchy, and the lineup is long past its classic best . . . Captain Kirk on keyboards. Dino Valenti's vocals have sounded stronger as well. But they hit on Bo at the end of the evening, and suddenly everything comes together, the guitar like the lights of far distant homesteads, the drums like the crackle of heat lightning on your skin, the bass is your heartbeat knowing something's behind you, and the keys are just a wash, awash with baleful breeze.

And it's still not the definitive version, because Quicksilver were

Old Absinthe House, New Orleans.

still on the road, still had a few of those 47 miles to walk. It's what's waiting at the end of that trek that really concerns us here, and, for that, we need to find Juicy Lucy.

Based in London but built around American slide guitarist Glenn Ross Campbell, Juicy Lucy formed from the wreckage of the Misunderstood, a California garage band that flared briefly but brightly enough to cut two of the most dramatic 45s of the entire psychedelic era, "I Can Take You to the Sun" and "Children of the Sun." "Who Do You Love" was in their repertoire as well, but while Quicksilver stretched it out into the archetypal California jam, all drawn-out drama and blistering instrumentation, the Misunderstood pumped it up but kept it short, psychedelic sound effects, heart attack drums, eerie harmonics . . . close, but no cigar. Campbell brought the song back for Juicy Lucy, but this time, they'd take the song back to where it began.

On a summer night in London, so many miles from the song's tempestuous origin, singer Ray Owen explained their version's nativity.

Owen's a fascinating guy, a black Londoner at a time when English rock was almost exclusively white. "We wanted to turn it around and make it a bit more exciting," he said. "The lyrics were pretty cool, but Bo can get pretty boring, no disrespect to him, so we wanted to make the song sound as exciting as the lyrics."

First, they stripped away every past reference to the song that they had ever heard, the early R & B bands that thumped it out on the club circuit, the extended psychedelia, and the booming druggie fallout. Owen took the lyrics and became the song's protagonist. You always got the feeling, listening to every other version of the song, that whoever was singing those lyrics didn't really believe what he was saying, that he was simply trying to impress the girl Arlene with a shopping list of the qualities that made him tougher than tough. Owen wanted to peel back the edges and see who Bo was really writing about.

"He's somebody who's really down to earth, who's had it rough and who sees life in a very straightforward way. He cuts away all the frilly stuff. He's done a bit of traveling, he knows how to cut out the bullshit and just get on with things. The person who sings those words has done all of that."

Owen's private vision of America at that time was not the one that a lot of British musicians of the period shared, of a fabulous wonderland where there are two cars for every boy, a Coke dispenser in every house and the sun shining down on a perpetual beach party. Nor, however, was it the world of graft and suffering that a lot of British bluesmen imagined, where men still worked the chaingang every day, and every Southern city was home to a thousand sad-eyed lowlanders, rocking away their last moments on the porch, looking forward to the day when they *wouldn't* wake up one morning.

America, to Owen, was none of these things. America to Owen was a land of darkness and mystery, where society and civilization were simply shards of light flickering fitfully over an impenetrable stygian heartland, a place where houses could indeed be made from rattlesnake skin, with towering chimneys constructed of human skulls, and where the ice wagon flew around pot-holed unpaved country roads, to drop off water or pick up the dead, whatever its customers needed.

It was a vision he had picked up from a thousand disparate sources; from music and literature, from movies and TV, but most of all from his own imagination, fired by the American friends and musicians whom he had met in London and on the road around England, and whose own home thoughts zeroed in on realities that the media of the day could only flash past.

He heard Professor Longhair pounding "Junco Partner" and pictured Angola Farm, the Louisiana state penitentiary where the boys were doing from one year to 99. Then he compared those thoughts to what Alan Lomax wrote about Parchman, across the line in Mississippi, how people died there and no one even noticed, playing out their jail sentences one day of hard labor at a time. Most modern bluesmen sang the words to the songs, but they never really comprehended what those words were actually saying, and even the authentic ones had had that meaning dulled by repetition.

He heard Marsha Hunt sing her chart-gnawing cover of "I Walk on Gilded Splinters," dancing on TV with full psych accompaniment and a dress that fired a raft of teenage hormones into overdrive, and he laughed at the kids who sang along, convinced that the chorus called out "tell Alberta." No, it sang, "'til I burn up," and there was a hell of a lot of difference, even if you didn't take it literally.

Ray Owen heard "Who Do You Love" in its multitudinous varieties, and decided to return the lyric, and its delivery, to the mouth of the man they were intended for. So when he arrived at IBC Studios in London that day in September 1969, nursing a ferocious head cold and convinced that he couldn't sing a single note, he was horrified to discover that recording would go ahead as planned, regardless of how dreadful he thought he sounded.

It was only afterwards, listening to the playback, that he realized that the cold was exactly what his performance required. It lowered the pitch of his voice, messed with the timbre and realigned his intentions, and it transformed the performance entirely.

The cold was cured, but Owen kept its tone, retraining his singing style so that every song now could revel in the fearful shadows that permeated "Who Do You Love"; he repaid the spirits that had come to his aid by penning a lyric for the band's first album that echoed Bo's bad boy from across the state line — the pounding "Mississippi Woman," with its textbook Deep South imagery and, underneath the sax break, the exact same mutant Diddley riff that David Bowie would later employ for "Jean Genie."

"Who Do You Love" was a U.K. hit in spring 1970; in America it meant little if anything, and that's a shame, because if any record poured its heart and soul into the nation's unseen psyche, it was Juicy Lucy howling through "Who Do You Love," all wailing guitars and slipping slide, a drumbeat that races your heart and a bass line that takes deep breaths for your lungs and, above it all, the conviction that it doesn't matter what is waiting for you just around the next corner, there's something even stranger around the one after that.

TRACK NINE

"Chateau Lafite '59 Boogie" by Foghat
from the LP *Rock and Roll Outlaws* (Bearsville Records)
1974

We parked the rental car on the edge of the Jean Lafitte National Historic Park and Preserve, on the shores of Lake Salvador, in the salty marshlands of Barataria — a place whose very existence screams resonance with a world that's far removed from this one.

Overhead, an airliner screams its way out of New Orleans International; in the distance, where Route 23 hugs the Mississippi down to Port Sulphur, trucks blare their horns. But Barataria slumbers on, and the only thought in your mind is, *where on earth did he put it?*

He being Jean Lafitte, and *it* being his treasure.

It feels strange in this day and age to think of pirate treasure being buried anywhere except on a sun-drenched desert island. But Jean Lafitte never visited any desert islands, or, if he did, he didn't think much of them.

Louisiana is lousy with piratical legends, and no surprise. Countless muddy inlets and bays allowed for all manner of illicit shenanigans to take place, and secreted all manner of hidey-holes for sundry felons to stash their loot in. It's true that few of the souls who took such advantage of this piece of natural largesse exactly

From 1720, an 18th-century view of the newly founded city.

conformed to the modern image of pirates, peg-legged Errol Flynn-alikes with parrots crying "pieces of eight," but they haunted the Spanish Main regardless, and were as fond of murder and mayhem as any son of Long John Silver could be.

Most of them were, anyway. But not Jean Lafitte. In fact, according to most of the tales that have come down, he was a gentleman first, a patriot second and a pirate a far distant third.

Lafitte was a Frenchman, born around 1780 either in France or else Saint Dominique, as Haiti was known at that time. When he was a child, however, his widowed mother relocated her family to New Orleans, where she remarried and her two children, Pierre and Jean, grew up.

The city limits were a lot tighter in those days; main streets literally gave way to wilderness, and houses and shops were poised on the very edge of swamp and lake. For a boy and then a young man growing up in New Orleans, the bayou could become as familiar as the city. So when Jean's older brother went to sea, and then returned as a successful privateer, operating out of Haiti and piled high with the treasures he collected on the waves, the younger sibling knew of as many places to hide them as he did places to sell them. In fact, by his mid-twenties, Jean was openly selling his brother's profits out of a store on Royal Street, and storing them in his own warehouse.

Well, that's one of the stories. There are others, giving Lafitte an autobiography of their own, but they all converge at one point: the passing of the Embargo Act of 1807, by which the American government prohibited its ships from docking at any foreign port. Louisiana had, by that time, been American territory for just three years; the state's entire fortune was built on maritime trade, legal or otherwise.

The ship owners faced a major loss in revenue, and one that could be balanced only by turning to crime in general, and to smuggling in particular. So they did. The Lafittes established a base in Barataria, far from the prying eyes of the government's law enforcement men, and were soon conducting as vibrant a trade as they ever could have in the past — more so, in fact, because when you evade one law, it becomes very easy to evade others, particularly those bothersome tariffs and taxes that the authorities love so much to levy.

But the brothers knew they could be doing even better, so in 1812 they purchased a schooner, hired a captain and, the following January, brought home their first prize: a Spanish vessel loaded with 77 slaves. Richer by $18,000, they converted the captured vessel into a second pirate ship, and, just weeks later, she not only brought home her first prize — $9,000 worth of cargo — but also established a reputation that Lafitte would treasure for the remainder of his career, as a gentleman pirate. There would be no unnecessary loss of life, no sinking captured ships for the fun of it — if he could not use his victim himself, he returned the vessel to its rightful crew and sailed on his merry way.

Soon, the Lafittes had a small navy at their disposal, with vessels both running a legal trade into New Orleans, and an illegal one into their base in Barataria, while the ongoing War of 1812 saw at least a portion of their pirating activities fall under the cover of legality, as the beleaguered United States issued letters of marque to any seafaring fellow who fancied taking his chances against the attacking British.

One of New Orleans' fabled jailhouses.

At the same time, however, Thomas Robertson, the newly installed acting governor of Louisiana, was taking a hard stand against pirates in general, and Jean Lafitte's men in particular, labeling them "brigands who infest our coast and overrun our country" and pledging his militia to bring them to justice. That his orders ran against public sentiment mattered nothing to Robertson — many of New Orleans' wealthiest and most influential families had something to thank the Lafittes for, whether it was the ease with which they could acquire certain goods, or some more personal favor. In 1814, Pierre Lafitte was arrested and charged with piracy.

Jean continued business as usual, but received notice that his activities were now internationally renowned: he received a hand-delivered message from the English king, King George I, offering Lafitte and his men British citizenship and land if they would only assist in the naval fight against the United States. Unfortunately, the flip of the coin was a second promise: if they refused the offer, the British would bombard Barataria back into the bayou.

Lafitte asked for 15 days in which to consider the offer; then, as soon as that was granted, he made copies of the communiqué and had them delivered to a sympathizer in the state legislature, together with a promise to do all he could to aid the Americans in their fight. All he asked in return was that brother Pierre be released from jail — and, two days later, the pair was reunited after what even the Lafitte sympathizers considered a very suspicious jailbreak. Yet, at the same time as the authorities begged Jean Lafitte for his assistance, they remained likewise committed to engineering his destruction, and, in one of the most perfidious exercises in American history, September 13, 1814, saw Commodore Daniel Patterson lead a full U.S. naval assault on the pirate's stronghold. Eighty of Lafitte's men were captured, together with eight vessels, 20 cannon and half a million dollars' worth of goods. A story published in the *Niles Weekly Register*, celebrating this "victory" ("a major conquest for the United States" were its precise words), described the military's foe as "a man who, for about two years past, has been famous for crimes that the civilized world wars against. . . ." Jean himself escaped, and, elsewhere around the world, and in the United States as well, public opinion was less easily impressed. Was this really how the infant republic intended repaying its heroes?

Neither would Patterson's victory remain unsoured. As the Battle of New Orleans drew nigh, and the city began to marshal its defenses against the oncoming British, it was discovered that the only able fighting force in the city were those same Baratarians that had been so ignominiously routed just weeks earlier, few of whom had any inclination to fight to defend their erstwhile attackers. Finally, a summit was held between the Americans commanding the city's defenses and Jean Lafitte, at which the wily pirate agreed to order his men into battle, provided they all received a full pardon.

This was granted, and all subsequent reports of the ensuing battle celebrate not only the heroism, but also the strategic knowledge of the pirates; it was Jean Lafitte who suggested extending the American lines into the swampland in which the invaders finally became becalmed; it was the Baratarians whose expertise with cannon and artillery prevailed against the less well-trained British. Lafitte was a

Pirate Alley, one of the ghostly LaFitte's favorite haunts.

hero, but, mindful of his past treatment, he was now wary of the perfidy of his Louisianan hosts. He shifted his base of operations along the coast to Texas; later, when that became too hot, he took up residence on the Cuban coast. He died in February 1823 when attempting to capture what he believed to be a pair of Spanish merchantmen, but which were actually heavily armed warships. He was buried at sea.

But of course he was not gone forever. Even during his lifetime, rumor abounded of the treasure that he had either buried, or otherwise stowed, in the swamps of Barataria — the untold riches that the Americans had never located, and which Lafitte had never found the time to return for. It is said that there is scarcely a spade's worth of ground, either there or elsewhere in coastal Louisiana (or farther afield, around Galveston) that has not been turned over by treasure hunters, who still go about their weary task, hoping to uncover what others may have missed.

Neither, in the years following his death, was there any shortage of reports of Lafitte himself being sighted, either as an extraordinarily persistent and mobile ghost (he is said to especially favor New Orleans' aptly named Pirate Alley), or even as a living being. It's not as if the national preserve that bears his name is any stranger to the supernatural, after all. Among a small army of shades to have been sighted round here, probably half of Lafitte's navy are reliably reported to still be at large, together with a woman with a dagger in her chest. And then there's Lafitte.

The circumstances of his death, after all, were believed by many to be cloudy enough to suggest that he didn't die in 1823, and where there's room for that original doubt, there is space for others as well — as certain followers of Elvis Presley, Jim Morrison and Michael Jackson can all testify today. And so we read of Jean Lafitte living on to achieve a grand old age; of him having a hand in all manner of bizarre and extraordinary escapades (including the rescue of Napoleon Bonaparte from his final exile); or even of him never dying at all, and living on today, secure within some bayou hideaway, simply awaiting the call to arms that will allow him to save his country once again.

Lafitte would be extraordinarily old, of course, but Louisiana is no stranger to that phenomenon. The fabled Fountain of Youth has long been believed to be hidden away in the Florida everglades — but one 15th-century swamp surely looked much like another. Maybe the original mapmaker just got his bayous confused. And I don't want to go all *Ripley's Believe It or Not* on you, but did you know that, until as recently as December 2008, the oldest man in the United States, George Francis, was a Louisianan? He was born in New Orleans on June 6, 1896 (the same date, curiously, as the oldest man in Britain, Henry Allingham) and lived to the ripe old age of 112 years and 204 days.

A living Lafitte, of course, would make Francis look like a toddler in comparison, but like King Arthur or Robin Hood, or any other hero who so firmly grasps an embattled nation's imagination, that is no barrier to immortality. And Lafitte *is* immortal, whether he is invoked in the name of the nature preserve that now marks the land that he called Barataria, or in the countless bars and hideaways that his old stamping grounds boast or the Contraband Days festival that celebrates him annually in Lake Charles, or the village hard up on the shores of Bayou Barataria that is itself called Lafitte.

Or even in a bottle of wine. Château Lafite-Rothschild has absolutely nothing to do with our pirate friend; it was named for an arm of the French judiciary that existed centuries before he was born. But what better glass could there be to raise to his memory, and what better song to listen to than the British blues band Foghat's celebration of a wild night on the tiles, "Chateau Lafite 59 Boogie"? Particularly as it clearly has nothing to do with wine (or pirates) in the slightest, but can knock back the whiskies with the best of them. Lafitte liked a drink, after all, and there's probably an ocean's worth of songs that he would sing when he'd had a few: the sailor's laments and chanteys that have filled every seaman's throat since the first man learned to ride the waves, the songs of piratical derring-do that seem so quaint to modern ears, but which were even harsher than reality to the men they rocked to sleep.

Lafitte himself has been celebrated in song since he buckled his very first swash, and he remains so today; the year 2008 saw no fewer than four well-stuffed CDs hit the shores, all released under the auspices of the Pirates for the Preservation of New Orleans Music and the titular pledge of *Lafitte's Return*, and every man jack of them littered with more buccaneers, ballads, scurvy knaves and well-spliced mainsails than Johnny Depp could shake his cutlass at.

TRACK TEN

"Bad Moon Rising" by Creedence Clearwater Revival
from the LP *Green River* (Fantasy)
1969

Lafitte's legacy did not die with him; it clings to these shores like Spanish moss, and haunts the imagination no matter how bright the day. How easy it is to place your mind's eye aboard a guileless merchantman, racing against its crew's own terrors to reach port before any prowling sea wolves caught up with it, and knowing that sundown left them as vulnerable as a well-baited hook? How easy it is, as well, to know that there is one song — or one thought, which could easily be translated into music — that sums up those terrors with room to spare. Because there are hurricanes a-blowing and rivers overflowing. . . . "Looks like we're in for nasty weather, cap'n, there's a bad moon on the rise."

Creedence Clearwater Revival's "Bad Moon Rising" is the end of the world set to music. It is every horror film you've ever seen, and every nightmare you've ever had. It might sound like a happy, bouncy pop song, all major chords and singalong choruses, but that's a big part of its brilliance. It hit the streets in August 1969 — the same week that half a million hippies were celebrating Woodstock, and half a dozen more were prowling the streets of Los Angeles, under direction of Charles Manson, slaughtering Sharon

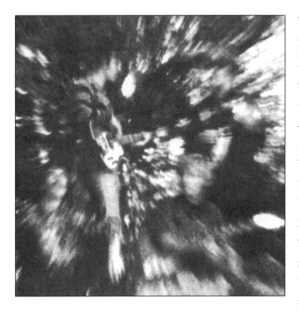

The shocking blur of Creedence Clearwater Revival's Bayou Country *LP.*

Tate and her friends. Today, "Bad Moon Rising" echoes through the soundtrack of *An American Werewolf in London*, and it works there; it rebounds through *Twilight Zone* (the movie, not the vastly superior TV show) and *Shaun of the Dead*, and it wrapped up the first season of *Supernatural*, where it also works well. In 1969, however, the song suggested something far more terrifying than the next scary moment in a movie. It intimated the end of the world, and as night falls over the bayou, that ending seems closer than ever.

No matter that toilet-bowl humorists and composer John Fogerty alike have been known to replace the "bad moon on the rise" with "there's a bathroom on the right." Watching any moon rise over the bones of Barataria, seeing it cracked by skeletal tree limbs, or beset by muddy clouds, with the salt in your nostrils and a light rain in your face, you suddenly realize why you packed so many Creedence songs onto your iPod. Because "Bad Moon Rising" is serious hoodoo, just as the band who cut the only significant version of it, Creedence Clearwater Revival, are serious Louisiana. John Fogerty was writing about the bayou long before he figured out why; as early as Creedence's second album, 1968's *Bayou Country*, he was dreaming in shades of dark green and darker, and kicking off the record with a slice of autobiography that could not have been truer if it had actually happened.

"'Born on the Bayou,'" he explained in a 1997 interview, "was . . . about a mythical childhood and a heat filled time, the Fourth of July. I put it in the swamp where, of course, I had never lived. I was trying to be a pure writer, no guitar in hand, visualizing and looking at the bare walls of my apartment.

"The feeling and everything was there first. We were on the stage at soundcheck at the Avalon Ballroom in San Francisco. I just started going into the lick, and I told Tom [Fogerty] to just keep hitting the E over and over. And I just started screaming syllables, sounds without any words. I worked the whole song without lyrics right there.

"I remember that Bobby Kennedy got killed during this time. I saw that late at night, live, and all night, because I had the TV on, they kept showing it over and over. 'Bayou' and 'Proud Mary' and 'Chooglin'' were all cooking at that time. I'd say that that was when the whole swamp bayou myth was born — right there in a little apartment in El Cerrito. I remember that I thought it would be cool if these songs crossed-referenced each other. Once I was doing that, I realized that I was kind of working on a mythical place."

John Fogerty insisted that the entire process was "totally unconscious. I didn't set out to do anything in particular. It just felt real good when I finished a song like 'Born on the Bayou.' I'd go, 'Yeah, I like that, I'd buy a record like that.'"

It sometimes surprises people to discover that Creedence Clearwater Revival had never been to bayou country when they first started singing its praises.

Brothers John and Tom Fogerty, bassist Stu Cook and drummer Doug Clifford started life as the Golliwogs, playing around the Bay Area scene at the same time, and on the same bills, as the Grateful Dead, the Jefferson Airplane and the Quicksilver Messenger Service. They cut a handful of singles for the Fantasy label, but when it came time to record their first album, label head Saul Zaentz laid down one relentless condition — they change their name. The Golliwogs was old hat now; it had been coined in an odd attempt to make the group sound more English at a time when the British invasion was in full swing. But those days were long gone; the kids wanted something trippier than that.

For a time, the quartet toyed with the notion of renaming themselves Muddy Rabbit. Gossamer Wump was another possibility, but they'd all been intrigued by one of Tom Fogerty's friends, a chap named Credence Newball, and the slightly misspelled Creedence Nuball was on their minds for a while. Close, but it still wasn't there. Finally, the group threw all caution to the wind. They kept the Creedence, but added Clear Water for a favorite beer, then threw on Revival to exemplify their renewed commitment to the band.

Plus, it sounded good.

Early Creedence had little in common with the most popular vision of San Francisco rock. They were no strangers to lengthy improvisations, but they worked them within the structure of a song, as opposed to an endless jam. They eschewed drug use, and the sly winking references to hallucinogenics with which their peers were prone to pepper their repertoires. And, whereas the best of the Frisco scene noodled introspectively, Creedence looked abroad for their inspiration — to the music that mattered before pop became paramount, and to the cultures that the modern world had worked so hard to destroy. Today, a similar worldview would be called Americana, and Creedence would have to join the queue of artists who've made that their mission in life. In 1967 and 1968, Creedence were unique. At least in rock 'n' roll terms.

All manner of slipstreams pass through Creedence's music, but country and blues are paramount, and it was the marriage of those with a rock 'n' roll sensibility that gave the band its most unique skein. Indeed, John Fogerty (the group's principal songwriter) once confessed that the best of Creedence's output, which includes "Bad Moon Rising," had its own genesis in an age when rock was itself still young.

"When a songwriter sits down to write a song, he may write 100 that are close, but not the exact song he was trying to get at," Fogerty said. "Bad Moon Rising" sounded like a 1950s rocker because that was when he started writing it. "I was trying to write that song for 10 years, and so when I started, it was the Presley era." In other words, back in the days when swamp rock was born, and now it was being reborn within a whole bagful of bands that looked to Creedence's clear-minded revivalism, and made the same tip of the hat.

From Taj Mahal and the Band to the Beatles' flat-top beckoning, holy-rolling "Come Together" and the Rolling Stones' "Midnight Rambler," they all had a taste of the bayou in their bones. . . . Step past the Midnight Rambler's genesis in the confessions of the Boston Strangler, after all, and he was the biggest, baddest bogeyman that anyone had seen since Staggerlee first disturbed the children's sleep. But Creedence out-swamped the lot of them.

The American South was the air that Creedence breathed, even before they visited it and certainly before it became a part of their musical landscape. At first, Fogerty explained, "I [simply] wanted the band to sound mysterious, to have its own definition, so I decided to mess around with 'Suzy-Q,' which was a cool rock 'n' roll song by Dale Hawkins. I kind of did the same thing with 'I Put a Spell On You.' Those songs took us to another place than where we'd been for 10 years." "Suzie Q" and "I Put a Spell on You" also became Creedence's first hit singles, in the dog days of 1968, but they were only the beginning.

Within six months, with "Proud Mary" and "Bad Moon Rising" also under their belts, Creedence were on course to outsell the Fab Four; in fact, one critic even called them the Bayou Beatles, an appellation that left Fogerty even more surprised that he should have been so obviously influenced by a geographic location that, at that time, he had never even visited.

Nevertheless, he told journalist Craig Werner, "People kept

pointing out [that my music] seemed so Southern, so swampy [and] I've thought about this for years. Where did that come from? Because I grew up in El Cerrito, California, and there wasn't much Southern about it."

And then one day it hit him. Look at the founding fathers of rock 'n' roll, jazz and the blues. They all came from the South. "Rock 'n' roll is Southern, and that's why I'm Southern. Because what I learned from was Southern. I rest my case."

Now it was simply a matter of zeroing in on which part of the South he wanted to "be" from. "I knew from the inside that I liked talking about swamps and spooky stuff. . . ." So he did.

The album that nailed Creedence's swamp credentials into place was their second, 1969's *Bayou Country* — another one, oddly, that *Rolling Stone* was less than enamored with, after the helter-skelter tumult that was their debut the previous year. "A few more fresh ideas would be helpful."

The title, of course, places the listener in a certain headspace, even before the music gets going, and journalist Greg Shaw probably nailed the whole thing in his 1971 reflection on the band for *Fusion* magazine: "the Southern influence became more pronounced and DJ's began babbling about 'swamp rock' whenever one of the many hit singles from it came up to play. 'Born on the Bayou' established the theme of the album, and introduced the pattern of riffs soon known far and wide as 'chooglin.'" "Keep on Chooglin'" even became everyone's favorite motto for a while. But Shaw also pointed out that the shift had started a couple of years earlier, during the last days of the band's career as the Golliwogs. "Walking on the Water," the B side of their final single, "You Better Get It Before It Gets You," stated a lot of what the band would soon become: crunching chords laid over a growling fuzz guitar, while Fogerty howled out the tale of a weird experience in a swamp by the river, watching a man who was walking on the water, hearing that man calling out his name, and putting into language a mood that had percolated in his mind all his life.

Or, as Greg Shaw continued, "The whole mythos developed out of John Fogerty's quite natural fascination with the South. His favorite music, blues and classic rock 'n' roll, had nearly all come from the South, and was full of references to it. He also had an interest in the folklore and culture of the South, and a sort of idealized vision of life along the bayous that proved a rich source of images which he used as metaphors to put across various messages in his songs."

Where the songs led, Fogerty's singing voice followed. Craig Werner explains, "Fogerty locates the accent that allowed him to cross over the Mason-Dixon line without providing proof of identity. There are some specific elements of the accent that place Fogerty in Louisiana, close to New Orleans, rather than, say, Memphis or Charleston. It's in the way he puts the Brooklyn twist on the vowels in the line 'woiking for the man every night and day,' the way he reduces the word 'bootleg' to the near-Cajun 'boolay.' No one ever really talked that way, but no one who came under Fogerty's spell was likely to notice, or mind."

Even today, with all the aforementioned competition, Creedence still sound startlingly unique. There are a lot of other bands that can stake a similar claim on similar influences, and a few whose acolytes might even do it better. But there's no one else who can come on the radio at two in the morning, hearing it through the grapevine, and transform the national anthem of soul music into something that seethes with so much unseen energy.

Of course, "Grapevine" is one of those songs that can lend itself to anything. In Gladys Knight's hands, it was the sweetest Tamla soul, and Marvin Gaye turned it into a pop classic. But the Temptations transformed it into barbershop funk, and, a decade later, the Slits manhandled it into dark roots reggae. Even the California Raisins had a stab at making it their own.

It was Creedence, however, who truly stripped it back to the foreboding basics that rumbled through the bass line that underpinned the whole song, and who then expanded it beyond belief, eight, nine, 10 solid minutes that coiled themselves around your soul, then took it out for the ride of a lifetime. No matter that the *Rolling Stone* review of the album from which it came, 1970's *Cosmos' Factory*, did not even mention the performance. From where anybody else's ears were sitting, "I Heard It through the Grapevine" *was* Creedence, and Creedence were everything you could want a band to be.

There are any number of songs that the band's fans would rate as their most archetypically swampy. "Who'll Stop the Rain," for example, or "Green River." Perhaps the richest of the images that John Fogerty conjured up from his adopted homeland, however, was "Proud Mary," the story of a Mississippi paddle steamer as she plies the waters from Memphis to New Orleans, a reminder of the days when the river was alive with traffic, and every smokestack told a tale. They were a long way from the pirates who plied those same waters, and whose sun had still to completely set even as the paddle steamers' morning began; and the goods that they hauled were a far cry from the nefarious treasures that once filled the river's cargo holds. But there was a spirit there that remained intact, of romance and rigor, of magic and mutiny, and most of all the indomitable power of storytelling.

The paddle steamers have starred in movies and books, and they are celebrated in more songs than many people could even begin to sing, although "Proud Mary" may not be all that she seems. At least according to some interpretations. Although the song does indeed tell of a young man who left a good job in an unnamed city, and made his way down to New Orleans, where he "hitched a ride on a riverboat queen," she was not necessarily called the *Proud Mary*. Not when there's a convenient piece of now-arcane (but then very contemporary) drug slang that renamed marijuana "Proud Mary Jane." Rolling on the river, indeed.

No, howl Creedence's own fans. If ever a band epitomized the anti-drug line in late '60s–early '70s American rock, it was Creedence

Clearwater Revival. Fogerty himself would explain that the song came about because he was working on three songs at the same time . . . "Proud Mary" about a washer woman, "Riverboat" about a paddle steamer, and "Rollin' on the River." None of them was anywhere near completion, but they blended well together, and *Proud Mary* was indeed destined to become the name of the paddle steamer.

Stagolee he was a bad man, ev'rybody know
He toted a stack-barreled blow gun and a blue steel
forty-fo'
Way down in New Orleans, dey call it de Lyon Club
Ev'ry step you walk in, you walk in Billy Lyons' blood.

Even as you walk up the gangplank, you really don't get a feel for what they must have been like in their prime. Paddle steamers, that is. You see them moored on the riverbank, glittering palaces of luxury, beckoning in the tourists to throw their money down on the tables, and maybe you can still grab a fission of the romance in which our culture has swathed the boats. Especially when the "crew" are all in period dress, and there's someone bashing out old-time favorites on the piano.

But you can't shake the knowledge, either, that it's all a hollow re-creation, some of it true, some of it legend, and all of it nicely polished and buffed to offer the *ultimate riverboat experience* (or whatever the promotional leaflets choose to call it), without a hint of the reality that was once their truth. The riverboat ride was about the excitement of actually going someplace. People didn't used to move around like they do today; you could spend your entire life in the same tiny town, and not feel at all hard done by, and if you did venture farther than the village down the road, that was a story you could dine out on for months.

Then the riverboats came, and suddenly the world opened up — an unknown, unimagined world of adventure and excitement. The best excitement they offer today, anchored to the quayside to wine and dine the sightseers, is when a mood-mangling supertanker passes off to the side, and her wash sends your Chardonnay slopping to the brim of the glass.

They were working boats, plying the river not for the idle curiosity of tourists, but to ferry the lifeblood of one city to the next, and the men and women who worked aboard them had a lot more to do than rake in the latest pile of chips that you lost.

And it so happened that one of these working boats gave her name to one of the most infamous killers in American folklore.

The paddle steamer *Stack Lee* was owned by the Lee Line, one of the multitude of steamboat companies that ferried passengers and goods from New Orleans to Memphis and back again around the middle of the 19th century. Like so many of their competitors, they offered their paying customers the best in river-borne luxury, comfort, speed, well-appointed cabins and tip-top cuisine. However, the crew who manned the vessels, kept the boiler stoked and stayed as far away from the passengers as they could were equally famously poorly paid — so poorly that there simply had to be some other incentive for them to work the back-breaking hours that a well-equipped paddle steamer would demand. There was. In 1939, folklorist Garnett Laidlaw Eskew published a near-century-old song that laid out in glittering detail the reasons why riverboatmen — particularly black riverboatmen, for some reason — enjoyed working for this employer.

Reason I likes de Lee Line trade
Sleep all night wid de chambermaid
She gimme some pie and she gimme some cake
An' I give her all de money dat I ever make.

The Lee Line, it seems, was also involved in prostitution, and why not? The steamship companies had a finger in a lot of pies back then.

It was the paddle steamers that tamed the American rivers in the first decades of the nation's life; more than that, it was the paddle steamers that opened up great tracts of the continent to its people. Until the arrival of the paddle steamer, it was muscle or wind that allowed man to get around, but both were finicky mistresses — muscles and animals, after all, tired, and while the wind might have been fine for crossing lakes (and even oceans), it was little help when ranged against the downstream currents of the mightiest rivers.

What we now see as an almost insignificant journey — St. Louis to New Orleans, for example, could take anything up to six months by land. Even the healthiest horses, after all, would be slowed by the appalling state of what then passed for roads, but which were little more than barely navigable trails. Then the paddle steamer came, and everything changed. Suddenly, that six-month journey could be completed in 20 days, and the race was on to make it even faster; by 1830, the trek had been cut to 12 days, and would soon be slimmed down to just three.

Although similar vessels had been operating on American rivers since the end of the 18th century, Robert Fulton, Nicholas Roosevelt and Robert Livingston (one of the fathers of the Louisiana Purchase) are generally credited as the founders of the Mississippi's paddle steamer tradition; they arrived in New Orleans with the so aptly named *New Orleans* in 1812. A stern-wheeler — so called because she was propelled by one great wheel at the stern of the vessel — the *New Orleans* was tiny by later standards; she measured just 116 feet in length, with a 20-foot beam and a one-cylinder engine, which was

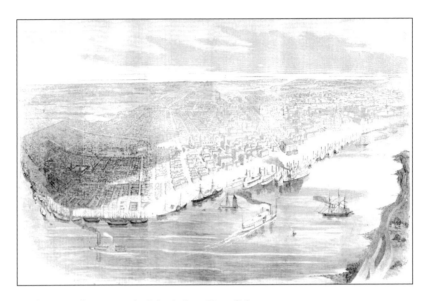

The growing sprawl of the infant New Orleans.

34 inches in diameter. She was a far cry, then, from the behemoth of a task that lay before her, but still Fulton saw her as the means of conquering the Mississippi.

As she undertook her maiden voyage on December 16, 1811, tied up at an island in the middle of the river, she was suddenly beset by a storm of unimaginable strength and magnitude — but it was not one that could have been predicted from the movement of clouds or weather patterns. This was a storm from below ground, the now-fabled New Madrid (Missouri) Earthquake, which devoured boats on the river as easily as it chewed up buildings on land and, for a time, even caused the Mississippi to run backwards. It was felt as far away as New Orleans in one direction, and Boston in the other. Somehow, the *New Orleans* made it through, a rare survivor on a day of such devastation, although her luck would not hold out forever. She would be lost in 1814, sinking on one of her regular runs between New Orleans and Natchez. But her example lived on.

Within five years, close to half a million tons of freight were being carried up and down the Mississippi by paddle-wheeled steamboats. Passengers, too, flocked aboard the vessels, confirming the craft's historical reputation as the single largest influence on the successful and expeditious opening of the lands that lay on the west of the Mississippi, not to mention the settlements that grew up along the Mississippi, Ohio and Missouri Rivers.

Among these vessels, and with the *New Orleans* now in her watery grave, the undisputed queen was the *Washington*, a double decked 403-ton vessel brought down by the Pittsburgh-based builder Henry Miller Shreve. He had already found favor with the locals after loading one of his earlier paddle steamers, the *Enterprise*, with ammunition and coming to the rescue at the Battle of New Orleans in 1814.

By the mid-1820s, over 100 different paddle steamers had been noted by the New Orleans Port Registry; by the 1840s, there were over 1,200 on the Mississippi. The paddle-wheeled steamboat remains the most potent symbol of man's conquest of the Mississippi — if conquest is even the correct word. It is more appropriate to call it a relationship, or even a romance, for that is what the steamers themselves represent: romance, glamour, history and magic all bound into one. Long after steam fell out of fashion as a means of propelling river traffic, the paddle steamers remained a part of local life, whether guiding tourists up and down the water, or offering them a convenient gambling den.

There were hundreds of paddle steamers plying the Mississippi to and from New Orleans, and hundreds of stories would attach themselves to them. Few, however, have passed into musical lore so thoroughly as the *Stack Lee*.

Was there a real Stack Lee who gave his name to the boat? Apparently so. According to Richard E. Buehler, writing in the *Keystone Folklore Quarterly*, "Many of the Lee Line boats were named for members of the Lee family, and one of them was Stacker Lee." Buehler then goes on to discuss another skein of history, and the fact

It was New Orleans' port that gave the city its wealth and its reputation, and the paddle steamers that carried both around the country.

that Edna Ferber took the name Stacker Lee for the eponymous heroine of her book, *Show Boat*, although here the vessel was named for a former Confederate soldier.

It doesn't really matter either way, for although the boat may not have been named for a man, a man was certainly named for the boat, and he became one of the most legendary figures in American folk songs — Stack Lee aka Stagger Lee aka Stag O'Lee aka Stackolee aka Stack-a-Lee aka just about every other variation on the same basic pronunciation.

And man oh man, he was bad.

The real Stack Lee, the one that the song was originally written about, was a two-bit murderer, and maybe a pimp, who was at large in the mid 1890s in St. Louis — not New Orleans, or any of the other cities into which his tale has been transposed. The *St. Louis Globe-Democrat* tells the story in the plainest terms: "William Lyons, 25, a levee hand, was shot in the abdomen yesterday evening at 10 o'clock in the saloon of Bill Curtis, at Eleventh and Morgan Streets, by Lee Sheldon, a carriage driver. Lyons and Sheldon were friends and were talking together. Both parties, it seems, had been drinking and were feeling in exuberant spirits.

"The discussion drifted to politics, and an argument was started, the conclusion of which was that Lyons snatched Sheldon's hat from his head. The latter indignantly demanded its return. Lyons refused, and Sheldon withdrew his revolver and shot Lyons in the abdomen. When his victim fell to the floor, Sheldon took his hat from the hand of the wounded man and coolly walked away. He was subsequently arrested and locked up at the Chestnut Street Station. Lyons was taken to the dispensary, where his wounds were pronounced serious. Lee Sheldon is also known as 'Stag' Lee."

Lee was arrested and tried, and while his first trial ended in a hung jury, he was not so lucky the second time around. He was found guilty and served time — just another bad man. But he became a folk hero too, assuming a character that went so far beyond any wickedness that he may have been guilty of in "real" life as to render him a virtual superman. He was, wrote Julius Lester in *Black Folktales*, "so bad that the flies wouldn't even fly around his head in the summertime, and snow wouldn't fall on his house in the winter."

Culture critic Griel Marcus goes even further. Stack Lee, he wrote, "is a story that Black America has never tired of hearing, and never stopped living out, like whites with their Westerns."

Eithne Quinn, author of *Nuthin' but a "G" Thang*, calls Stack Lee "[one of] the most influential bad man forebears of gangsta rap," while Black Panther leader Bobby Seale even named his son after him — Malik Nkrumah Staggerlee Seale.

"Beautiful name, right? He's named after his brother on the block, like all his brothers and sisters off the block: Staggerlee. Staggerlee is Malcolm X before he became politically conscious. Livin' in the hoodlum world. You'll find out. Huey [Newton] had a lot of Staggerlee qualities. I guess I lived a little bit of Staggerlee's life too, here and there. . . . And at one time, brother Eldridge [Cleaver] was on the block. He was Staggerlee. And so I named that brother, my little boy, Staggerlee, because — that's what his name is."

Stack Lee is the archetypal bad guy, then, but he's also the archetypal rebel, the archetypal spanner in the works, the archetypal fist in the face of whoever tries to fuck with you. "Don't come around my house, or I'll send Stack Lee round to yours" was once among the most chilling threats a man could utter . . . or have uttered to him, but what did it mean?

It meant, if he was lucky, that he might simply be shot like poor William Lyons. And if he was unlucky . . . well, the song, like the story, has undergone myriad variations in the century-plus since it was first coined, in which Stack has metamorphosed into everything from an avenging angel to the Devil himself — or, at least, a man whom the Devil had heard of, and maybe wished that he hadn't. At least one version of the song includes a line about Old Nick hearing a mighty rumbling under the ground, and ascribing it to another bout in Stack and Billy's battle, while another suggests that it was the Devil who provided the distinctive Stetson that Stack is usually depicted as wearing, made from the rawhide of a man-eating panther that Satan himself had skinned alive. Baron Samedi would have been proud of the workmanship.

The earliest known version of Stag's saga set to music was recorded in 1923 by Frank Westphal & His Regal Novelty Orchestra, but it had already been around for a while. When hillbilly Frank Hutchinson recorded it in 1927, he declared that he'd learned it from a black cripple named Billy Hunt, and the authenticity of this particular tale might be borne out by Bob Dylan, who himself cut a flirtatiously foreboding rendering of the song in 1993, adapted wholly from Hutchinson's original take.

By 1928, "Staggerlee" had become a jazz standard, courtesy of Duke Ellington, and when Alan Lomax went out on his travels, he collected any number of retellings of the murder and its meanings, many of which read more like 18th-century broadsides and chapbooks than any simple remembrance of a not-so-remarkable bar-room killing. In later years, the Clash would excerpt the adventure in their own "Wrong 'Em Boyo," and create a whole new cautionary legend.

Lomax paid his first visit to Louisiana in 1934, traveling out into bayou country to record a unique document of the regional sound, largely comprising unaccompanied ballad singers and solo instrumentalists. Many of these songs and styles were old even then, brought to the region by the successive waves of settlers that shaped the area, and within whose social melting pot the distinct Cajun and Creole cultures were forged. Lomax returned three years later, to discover that songs he had long since assigned to other regions (or even countries) entirely were not immune from local influence.

The story of Stack, for instance. He may not have been a local boy, but Louisiana adored Stack, and the reasons why should now be obvious. Indeed, New Orleans had already adopted Stack for itself, and had both a musical and an oral history to back up its ownership, as evidenced by the version in which the song's eponymous hero ("a bad man, ev'body know") "toted a stack-barreled blow gun and a blue steel forty fo' . . . down to Rampart Street," to shoot Billy Lyon "three times in de forehead and two times in de side."

It isn't the only traditional folk song to have been snatched away like that. The equally potent "St. James Infirmary" is actually descended from an Irish folk song, and is usually numbered among the great canon of Texan cowboy ballads (which is why you should hunt out an amazing version by Australia's Triffids). "St. James Infirmary" has long been considered a local standard, ever since the young Jelly Roll Morton was hanging out on the corner of Marais and Bienville, in the heart of the Storyville district, watching the sick and injured being ferried to the makeshift first aid service that was once provided by St. James Methodist Church. In the rock era, versions by Dr. John (of course) and, more recently, Allen Toussaint have seen the song retain that local flavor; likewise, Dr. John was only one of the state's favorite sons who committed Stack's tale to vinyl.

A local barrelhouse pianist named Archibald Cox led his

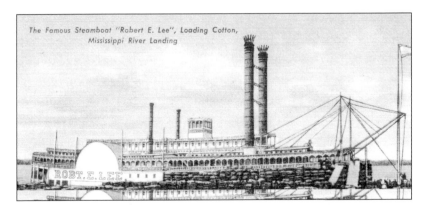

The Famous Steamboat "Robert E. Lee", Loading Cotton, Mississippi River Landing

One of the most famous of all the paddle steamers, the Robert E. Lee.

orchestra to an R & B Top 10 spot in 1950 with the saga, tracing it not only to its usual conclusion, with poor Billy lying and dying in the bar, but on to a whole new denouement, as Stag staggers wounded from the scene of the crime, then drops down dead at his own mother's door. From there, of course, he descends into hell, where the Devil is waiting with an unusual request, for Stag to identify his dead victim's soul. They immediately start to fight again, until the Devil finally separates the pair, then places them smack next to each other on the shelf where he keeps all his souls.

Not only did Cox return the song to the charts, though, after an almost three-decade absence, he also inadvertently helped old Stag cement the shared heritage that unites Jamaican ska with New Orleans R & B, when Prince Buster took his love of Cox's pounding version and rerecorded it for a Kingston, Jamaica, dancehall smash.

Ostensibly, Buster's version of the song was a tribute to the American R & B radio that blared in from New Orleans while he was growing up, and which proved a formative influence on the early days of ska. But there was more to it than that. The mid-1960s saw Jamaica in the grip of the Rude Boys, a youth cult that, in the eyes of the establishment, set the high-water mark in juvenile delinquency. Everything from random graffiti to street crime to murder was laid at the door of the Rude Boy fraternity, but so was the gallivanting popularity of the island's most outspoken music stars. Prince Buster was just one of several leading performers whose music spoke directly to the Rude Boy community . . . the then-little-known Bob Marley and the Wailers were numbered among the others. Before Prince Buster even set about writing his own musical tributes to Rudie tenacity (the "Judge Dread" trilogy of 1966–67), he seized upon Stag as a role model for them all. Buster's rendition of the hoary old tale may not be the most sinister or violent of Stag's multitudinous incarnations. But it's certainly the most politically charged.

Another New Orleanian, singer Lloyd Price, took the song even further afield. Drafted to Korea by the military, he put together a band with some of his fellow draftees and toured the army bases with an act built at least in part around the story of Stack Lee.

"There were hundreds of lyrics for the old song, but no story. While entertaining the troops, I had put together a little play based on it," Price said. "I'd have soldiers acting out the story while I sang it." He shrugged off accusations that he had simply rewired Archibald Cox's version (a belief that Cox, at least, was so convinced by that he took legal action to prove it). Price pointed out that there were dozens of variations on the song at large by then, and a lot of them were sung in New Orleans. What he did was bring the best of them together.

Whatever the truth, Price's version went down a storm every night, the motif of murder, mayhem and vengeance one with which almost every conscript in the crowd could identify. Back on civvy street, once the army let Price go, the acclaim was just as vociferous.

Price recorded the song in 1958 and shot to the top of the R & B charts, and then the pop listings too. At one point, "Stagger Lee" was selling 200,000 copies a day and incurring the wrath of none other than Dick Clark as it did so. Faced with Price on the guest list for his show, and knowing that Stag would be along for the ride, Clark announced that he would not allow Price to perform it on air unless he first recorded a version that was littered with less blood and guts.

Price complied and emerged from the studio with the only happy ending that Stag had ever known, in which he and Billy Lyons become friends again.

Elsewhere, however, as the song and its subject sank deeper into urban culture, so did the sheer outrage of the seething Stack's exploits. He became a rapist, a serial killer, a patricide, a mass-murderer — although for sheer mindless, violent nastiness, masquerading as a track on one of the best-loved hit albums of 1996, you need to dig very deep to underwhelm the Nick Cave and the Bad Seeds centennial rendering of the epic, from his U.K. Top 10 hit album *Murder Ballads*.

One of the most dramatic versions of the song, and certainly the one that most influenced Cave's retelling, can be found in *The Life: The Lore and Folk Poetry of the Black Hustler* by Dennis Wepman, Ronald B. Newman and Murray B. Binderman (1986). Collected from a New York prison inmate named Big Stick, it took its own lead and language from the braggadocio-laden retellings of the saga that were common lore on the street, brutal barrages in which even the bar was renamed as the Bucket of Blood, and every word out of Stag's mouth was either an insult or a cuss.

Impressed by the sheer descriptive rage of the lyric, Cave had the band improvise a backing track on the spot, then threw himself at the mike and into the performance, becoming Stag with such blinding precision that when he announces *"I'm* Stagger Lee!" you don't question him for a moment. It's a little like Alex Harvey announcing the arrival of Amos — you hear the words, but you see them as well.

"Stagger Lee appeals to me simply because so many people have recorded it," Cave told *Mojo* magazine in 1996. "The reason we did it, apart from finding a pretty good version in this book, was that there is already a tradition. We're kind of adding to that."

And what were they adding?

Cave laughed. "The final act of brutality, where the great Stagger Lee blows the head off Billy . . . while he is committing fellatio [was] especially attractive," although that was not all. "There's a verse to our version that goes, 'I'm the kind of cocksucker that would crawl over 50 good pussies to get to one fat boy's asshole,' which I heard on an amazing talking blues song by a guy who, in the song, introduces himself as Two-Time Slim. I've always thought that was a groovy line, so I just threw it in for good measure." And Cave concluded, "I like the way the simple, almost naive traditional murder ballad has gradually become a vehicle that can happily accommodate the most twisted acts of deranged machismo. Just like Stag Lee himself, there seems to be no limits to how evil this song can become."

Stack, doubtless, would have applauded that sentiment, and prophecy, as loudly as anyone.

TRACK
TWELVE

"Louisiana 1927" by Marcia Ball

from the LP *Notodden Blues Festival — Bluestown* (Bluestown)

2005

If the Mississippi River had not existed, Mark Twain would have had to invent it. The author formerly known as Samuel Longhorne Clemens was born in Florida, Missouri, in 1835, and grew up in nearby Hannibal, a port town that fueled his love for the Mighty Mississippi. At one point, after taking a paddle steamer journey to New Orleans, Clemens even wanted to become a riverboat pilot, an occupation that could pay up to $250 a month — a staggering wage for the time. He would spend the next two years of his life studying for his pilot's license and, in so doing, became intimately acquainted with every port, wood lot, shoal and obstruction that the river had to offer.

He also learned of the Mississippi's cruel side. In 1858, Clemens convinced his younger brother Henry to join him on the river, only for the boy to be killed when the vessel he was working on, the *Pennsylvania*, exploded — a common tragedy in those days of vast and frequently decrepit or ill-repaired metal boilers and often over-worked boilermen. Indeed, America's worst ever maritime disaster — the explosion and loss of the SS *Sultana* in April 1865, as she journeyed from New Orleans to St. Louis packed with some 2,400 recently released union POWs — was caused by just such a mishap. Rather than wait three days for a faulty boiler to be replaced, the vessel's captain, J. C. Mason, simply had it patched. Six days later, the boiler blew. Three-quarters of the people onboard the ship, in excess of 1,800 souls, were killed in the ensuing conflagration.

Clemens received his pilot's license the year after his brother's death, but he never put it to much use. Instead he wrote, and in so doing, he navigated the Mississippi with even greater finesse and expertise than he might ever have managed from behind a ship's wheel.

The Mississippi enters Louisiana just above Lake Providence and forms the state line all the way south to Torras. Then the neighboring Magnolia State veers sharply and precipitously off to the east, following the lines drawn by the Spanish withdrawal of 1798, and the river rolls on down through Baton Rouge and New Orleans to finally empty into the Delta.

Its mouth has been moving all that time. Four and a half millennia ago, the river entered the country in roughly the same place as Morgan City now stands. Fifteen hundred years later, it had relocated to Chalmette; 700 years ago, what is now the Bayou Lafourche was the mouth of the Mississippi; and, for the past 400 years — that is, for as long as we've been keeping records of such things — it has opened at the aptly named Pilot Town.

The Mississippi is the lifeblood of the state, of course, the artery that kept trade and commerce, life and limb, man and beast alive for as long as such things have clung to life in the region; and the source, too, of as much myth and legend as any other feature in the state.

Big Muddy has known many names. To the first Spaniards to visit the area, it was the Río del Espíritu Santo, the River of the Holy Spirit, although they later took to referring to it as Río Palizado, in honor of the vast mud formations that, from a distance, looked like palisades. But the earliest Spanish explorers never really ventured into what became Louisiana, preferring to stick to the river until they came to what we now call Arkansas City, and then carving a march into modern-day Texas with a circuitous meander that wanted nothing to do with the vast, tractless swampland that lay to their south. For them, the river was as wet as they'd get, at least until they'd declared the boundaries of their empire.

The Frenchmen Louis Joliet and Father Jacques Marquette, who explored the Mississippi in 1673, renamed the waters Conception; their countryman LaSalle retitled it for the then incumbent French Minister of Finance, Jean-Baptiste Colbert; and when New Orleans was settled, the river became the Fleuve St. Louis, after the sanctified king.

But it was the Ojibway Indian name for the river that would survive. Or was it the Algonquin? Different sources seem certain that they are correct, but there's one thing they do all agree on. They called it the Great River: Missi Sipi. Maybe, however, we should pay less attention to what the river *is*, and more to what it conceals.

Bleached churches framed in Spanish moss. Dilapidated fishing boats tied precariously to decaying wooden docks that probably stood in danger of collapse on the day they were built, and which countless new years have only weakened even further. Peeling paint and sun-scorched skin. Accents and dialects that were already old when the New World was young. And, pervading it all, as thick as the fishermen's arms or their lady friends' waists, the air.

You don't breathe the air here — you drink it, and, with every breath, you can feel your lungs turn to gills as they strive to adapt to the alien world within which you have stranded them. Our planet's atmosphere, we are taught, is comprised of 78 percent nitrogen, 21 percent oxygen and a one percent cocktail of sundry other gases. Down here, though, you wouldn't bet on that being true. There's methane and marsh gas, oil and gasoline, damp and decay, wet wood and rotting undergrowth, and the sweat is so thick on your skin that it could pass for a second skin, if it wasn't for the sheen of dirt that itches beneath it.

Rough, old meanie that he was,
From Spain came Don Gorez Goz.
As he cast a wary eye about
A pretty lass espied this lout.

He bought her—this Indian maid—
For a cake of soap, a yard of braid.
The grieving beauty fled with cause
For tarnished braid indeed it was.

Gorez pursued both hard and fast
Until she climbed a tree at last.
As Gorez followed her he leered.
How those branches caught his beard!

The beard remains, but Gorez has gone
And still the tale goes on and on.
What an ominous warning it should be
To see Spanish Moss hang from a tree.

A cake of soap and a yard of braid
May be enough to win some maid.
Look, though, swain, and make thou sure
The braid is clean, untarnished—pure!
—P. M. L.

And the worst of it is, unless you're working from a really recent map, you don't even have a sound sense of where you actually are.

In 2003, writing in his memoir *Bayou Farewell*, author Mike Tidwell noted that the bayou was disappearing at a rate of a football field's worth of land every 20 minutes. Three years later, in *Whalebone Strict*, author Lady Alice McCloud caught the same air of decay. "A tiny channel, invisible from just a few yards away . . . a wooden cabin [standing] among a grove of some sort of cypress, with an elderly mule tethered at the front. A rotting jetty . . . [its] planking warped and split with long exposure to the sun." Once, the channel would have been openly navigable, the jetty pristine and flat as a pancake.

And all this in the twinkling of an eye, or at least the passage of a few generations.

Less than 100 years ago, great swaths of the Delta were cotton country. When the Second World War broke out, it was prime orange-growing land. By the turn of the 20th century, though. . . .

Maybe you remember the night that Katrina hit: how, even as great slices of New Orleans began to vanish beneath the waves, the TV news was still celebrating how deftly the city had dodged the hurricane-force bullet. Now travel 90 miles almost due south and picture what it was like down there.

We're following firmly in Tidwell's footsteps here, with *Bayou Farewell* for a road map, and the small town of Leeville as the landmark we're shooting for. We're all the way down at the tip of Lafourche Parish, overlooking the Timbalier Bay, true Delta country, and if you haven't read the book, you should.

On the one hand, it's a cautionary tale, overflowing with reminders of just what an asshole man can be, particularly once he has caught the scent of petro-dollars or property values. And on the other, it's a wake, because the slow farewell that Tidwell foretold, of a man-made apocalypse slowly choking the life from the people here, was hastened and even hammered into place by the storm that even the weatherman never accurately foretold. Back in the 1970s, when man and musician dreamed of Armageddon, it tended to be an atomic apocalypse that was going to send us all to hell in a handcart — "the Louisiana Delta where the Mississippi's dried up," warned British space rockers Hawkwind in 1977's "Damnation Alleyway," and few listeners even dreamed of a day when quite the opposite might come true.

The city lost houses; Leeville lost the land that the houses were built on. Grand Isle, where the storm made landfall that night of August 29, 2005, was just the other side of the narrow peninsula upon which Leeville sits, and it wasn't only the ground that was inundated. Louisiana Route 1 is the only means of land access to Port Fourchon, which services 16 to 18 percent of our nation's domestic and imported oil and gas. It is the only means of land access to the Louisiana Offshore Oil Port (LOOP), which handles 14 percent of U.S. imported crude oil, and the only means of evacuation for approximately 35,000 people, including 6,000 offshore workers. For these and countless other reasons, Route 1 is one of the most critical highways in the South. And it had been transformed into a lake.

Great stretches of the rusty old Leeville Bridge, a two-lane drawbridge that was already past its prime, were under water as well,

*A scene from the 1927 flood, over
Greenville, Mississippi.*

and when the tides receded, they just left more water. Grocery stores that had once teemed with people now had only fish for customers, and a half-submerged cemetery that gave Mike Tidwell such a start in 2003, perched just off the tip of Bayou Lafourche, had more or less vanished completely.

I opened his book and thumbed to the page. "A dozen or so old tombs," he wrote, "tumbling brick by brick into the bayou water. The rectangular three-foot sarcophagi each entombing a single human being above the ground in the South Louisiana style, look like slow motion lemmings dropping over the fateful edge." When he was there, the only visitors it received were the fishermen who came to cast for the creatures that had made new homes in the underwater brickwork. Half a decade on, even the fishermen are disappearing. No longer is it worth their while to perch themselves on half-sunken sarcophagi, to catch the fish that swim around the debris and the dead, because the fish themselves are becoming fewer and fewer, as the entire area is slowly transformed into one vast and unlivable salt marsh. There are no fish in the Dead Sea, either.

So no, a map doesn't help because, as soon as one is drawn, the waters claim another landmark. You could be any place, any time, and as your body acclimatizes to the unfamiliar air, so your mind scrambles to comprehend something else. No cell phone towers. No chain stores. No edge-of-town malls. No blocks upon blocks of car dealerships and fast-food eateries. No Best Buy or Walmart or

Borders or Acme. Your laptop battery could die out here, and nobody would even care. Too much else is dying alongside it.

Junior, Louisiana, in the aftermath of the 1927 flood.

This land was shaped by two forces. First there was nature, the waters of the Mississippi, winding its way from the north, and the storms that blow in from the Gulf of Mexico, to the south. This is the point where they meet, a shattering collision of unbreakable power, one to level the land, the other to drench the debris.

It was the river that created the bayou, flooding the land since the beginning of time, piling up sediment, shifting the soil, creating the natural levees and landfills that shaped a way of life, and kept the waters of the gulf from inundating the earth. That was just the way it worked, and when the first settlers arrived here — exiles mainly from elsewhere on the continent, shunted down to the rump of the land because they simply lived in a manner that disturbed their neighbors, they found a natural floodplain rich in life. So they tried to stop it from flooding.

They built dams and levees, and some of them held. Townships grew, cities took root, and, though the waters would always come back to reclaim the soil that had been snatched away from them, they were an aggravation, rather than a curse. You learned to live with the floods because you wanted to live with everything else.

Until the spring of 1927.

Nine months of unnaturally heavy rains had filled the Mississippi

New Iberia, 1927.

beyond bursting point. Its tributaries flooded first, as far away as Kansas and Iowa. In Tennessee, the Cumberland River poured over levees that towered more than 50 feet high. But it was the Mississippi that everybody was watching, and when it broke its man-made shackles, it broke them big-time.

On Good Friday, April 15, 1927, the *Memphis Commercial Appeal* newspaper cautioned its readers that "the roaring Mississippi River, bank and levee full from St. Louis to New Orleans, is believed to be on its mightiest rampage."

The paper warned of, although it didn't quite predict, "the greatest flood in history," and that morning its words were proven true. Biblical rains of record-breaking proportions hammered the states of Missouri, Illinois, Arkansas, Mississippi, Texas and Louisiana. New Orleans recorded 15 inches of rain in 18 hours; eye witnesses described the river as raging like an ocean, with a tumult that destroyed everything in its path.

The official word was not to panic. A system of levees that had been constructed in previous years by the United States Army Corps of Engineers would assuredly hold, insisted the authorities, with the floodwaters being diverted down the channels that were intended to take them, into Atchafalaya River, into Lake Pontchartrain, into the Gulf of Mexico. And just to be sure, emergency teams were sent out to raise the height of the most vulnerable levees.

Their efforts made no difference. If the turbulent river could not crest the dams, it simply broke through them, worked around them or burrowed beneath them. Water up to 30 feet deep in places covered an area the size of Vermont, New Hampshire, Massachusetts and Connecticut combined. And the rains kept on pouring.

One hundred and forty-five levees gave way, and 27,000 square miles of land were under water. Up in Memphis, the Mississippi measured 60 miles wide at one point. And down in Louisiana, there was no point in even trying to measure it, not after the Caernarvon levee was dynamited, in an attempt to save New Orleans from the waters, at the expense of every place else.

To the south of the city, Saint Bernard Parish was all but obliterated in the ensuing deluge. Everything east of the river in neighboring Plaquemines Parish was gone, too. Over a thousand people died in the flood and almost a million were displaced.

"Picture to yourself this great inland sea," wrote author Lyle Saxon in his *Father Mississippi*. "Mile upon mile of muddy water, with never a bit of dry land anywhere; houses askew, roofs fallen in, and the water filled with dead animals."

As Saxon passed through the disaster zone, that broad swath of now inundated land that separates the Mississippi from the Red River, he saw chickens and snakes roosting in the same trees, mindless of one another, caring only to escape the waters. "Abandoned dogs bark pitifully from housetops . . . and everywhere, rising above the water, are half-submerged trees, pink crepe-myrtles, blossoming magnolias, the creamy blossoms beginning to turn brown already from the surrounding waters."

Saxon watched once-prized household objects bob past his little boat, and wondered what stories the detritus could tell — who owned it, who lost it, who would mourn for it later, when the waters had receded and life had returned? Because it would return, and, what's more, it would be better than ever before. For, amidst all the political hand-wringing and expressions of regret with which every natural disaster is naturally met, there came the announcement that

Bird Life on the Louisiana Gulf Coast

Young Pelicans

Picturesque LOUISIANA

it would never happen again. Never again would Grandma's patchwork quilt be swept away on a raging tide; never more would Marylou's favorite doll be washed out of her screaming grip; never again would the general store be sent floating down Main Street as the angry currents ripped its foundations away.

It was the Flood Control Act of 1928 that unleashed the United States Army Corps of Engineers once more on the problem, with the solution already in hand. They would construct the world's largest and most impenetrable levee system, one which ran the length of the lower Mississippi. New man-made floodways would divert excess water out of harm's reach. There would not be an inch of even theoretically vulnerable land that was not safeguarded by one ingenious device or another. By 1936, the Mississippi River had 29 locks and dams, hundreds of runoff channels, and a thousand miles of levees. There would still be floods, some catastrophic. But, for the most part, the river wasn't simply tamed, it was all but emasculated.

So the river stopped flooding, but that meant it also stopped building. Every time the Mississippi crossed its own banks, it would bring with it a mountain of soil and sediment to spread across the land around it, to replace that which natural erosion had worn away. Stop the flood and you stop the sediment. Stop the sediment and you start to sink. And it doesn't take an army engineer to tell you what happens next, especially if you happen to be standing on the coast. Because the land might be sinking, but the sea level isn't.

In fact, it's rising at such a rate that the only thing that changes more than a modern map of the bayou are the futuristic projections of how the American coastline might look once global warming has really sunk its teeth into the ice caps. One recent effort drew a straightish line from Baton Rouge west to Lake Charles, and east above Covington, and called that the United States' future gulf coast. Everything below that will be fish food.

The flood of 1927 was quick to find its way into folklore, not only in Louisiana but the length of the Mississippi. Wherever the waters affected a community, the community remembered the devastation. Today, however, popular awareness of the disaster concentrates upon one particular battle as emblematic of the battles that took place all along Big Muddy's course: the fight to save the Mississippi state town of Greenville. Memphis Minnie's "When the Levee Breaks," granted worldwide fame by Led Zeppelin, was itself set in Greenville.

But that's all Greenville is, an emblem, a single example of sheer public heroism somehow winning out over official incompetence, for Greenville was ultimately lucky. It stayed relatively dry. Farther south, the people told a tragically different story.

By May 2, 1927 — that is, 17 days after the first levees shattered — five grossly swollen rivers were pouring across nine Louisiana parishes. Four breaks in the embankment south of Vidalia sent the Mississippi hurtling across Concordia Parish; east of Alexandria, in Avoyelles Parish, the Red River smashed through its northern bank. The Arkansas River had overcome the defenses of Jones and Bonita in Morehouse Parish and sent over a thousand refugees rushing to Bastrop. The same river's waters reached into Tensas Parish, inundating two miles of the Missouri Pacific Railroad tracks above

A view from the Mississippi in the mid-1980s.

Newellton. In Richland Parish, the water was reported to be six feet deep at Bardel. And so on. Cotton and sugar cane plantations were flooded; oil and gas production was shut down.

In 1974, songwriter Randy Newman composed his own memorial to the flood, and turned the spotlight fully upon the hardest hit of all the river's victims. "Louisiana 1927," he explained to the *New York Times*, was originally inspired by his love of the state's history, and his own deep-seated roots within its borders.

"I was born in Los Angeles, but I went to New Orleans when I was a week old, my mother's from there, my family's still there." As he grew up, "it was the place I knew"; he spent several summers there, and a longer spell while his father was away during the Second World War. He fell in love with the city — "it's carefree, it's careless ... it's not the sort of place you go to get your car fixed," he once memorably quipped, although he also admitted that, even as a child, "there were these horrendous things — those signs with 'Colored' on one side and 'White' on the other. But I always loved the pop music. I was so influenced by Fats Domino that it's still hard for me to write a song that's not a New Orleans shuffle.

"I was interested in the history and I'd heard about the flood, so I wrote the song," Newman said. He recorded it alongside a tribute to Governor Huey Long, "Kingfish," on the 1974 LP *Good Ol' Boys*. It was Long who led the campaign of retribution against the businessmen who tugged on sundry local corrupt purse strings to ensure that New Orleans was saved from the flood at the crippling expense of its less illustrious neighbors, only to then discover that the city would probably have been alright after all.

Newman's song took a while to permeate into the national, or even the regional, consciousness, although that is not to say it wasn't appreciated. "The Ambrose Bierce of rock 'n' roll . . . revives the Southern motif of [his earlier hit] 'Sail Away' updated 200 years," mused *Rolling Stone*'s Stephen Davis. "Now the South is wrecked and shamed. . . ."

But it wasn't until Linda Ronstadt mentioned the song to Aaron Neville, with whom she was recording at the time, that "Louisiana 1927" truly caught the imagination. In 1991, Neville included a ferocious orchestra- and choir-swamped version of the song on his CD *Warm Your Heart*, imbuing it with all the drama and horror that Newman's own, self-confessedly understated vocal could never have attained. "And," continued the *New York Times*, "because he was closely identified with New Orleans in a way that Mr. Newman never was, he gave that chorus a first-person authenticity."

From Neville, the song spread throughout the city. Bo Dollis and the Wild Magnolias recorded it in 1996, but updated it to restage the drama of 1965, the onslaught of Hurricane Betsy. Marcia Ball took the song on in 1997, and brought a whole new aspect of heartbreak to it, even before the entire state adopted it as an unofficial anthem in 2005, in the wake of Hurricane Katrina. "When I used to sing that song, it was about something that happened a long time ago," Aaron Neville admitted. "Now when I sing it, it's about something that happened to me and my family, so it's a lot more real."

"For a long time after Katrina," agreed Ball, "there just wasn't a dry eye in the house when I did that song."

The fear of flooding was not man's only reason for messing with the river, of course. Its length and shape, too, exercised the imagination and ingenuity of sundry gentlemen, as Mark Twain pointed out in his *Life on the Mississippi*.

*When the river is rising fast, some scoundrel whose planta-
tion is back in the country, and therefore of inferior value,
has only to watch his chance, cut a little gutter across the
narrow neck of land some dark night, and turn the water
into it, and in a wonderfully short time a miracle has happened: to wit, the whole Mississippi has taken possession
of that little ditch, and placed the countryman's plantation
on its bank (quadrupling its value), and that other party's
formerly valuable plantation finds itself away out yonder
on a big island; the old watercourse around it will soon
shoal up, boats cannot approach within ten miles of it, and
down goes its value to a fourth of its former worth. Watches
are kept on those narrow necks, at needful times, and if a
man happens to be caught cutting a ditch across them, the
chances are all against his ever having another opportunity to cut a ditch.*

Other cuts were made to ease shipping times. Twain again: "the
Mississippi between Cairo and New Orleans was 1,215 miles long 167
years ago. It was 1,180 after the cut-off of 1722. It was 1,040 after the
American Bend cut-off. It has lost sixty-seven miles since. Consequently its length is only 973 miles at present."

It was one of these operations that gave rise to one of Louisiana's
most enduring river legends, that when the Raccourci cut-off
reduced the river's length by 28 miles, one of the Mississippi's trade-
mark paddle steamers became trapped in the cut-off itself. On foggy
nights, it is said, the vessel can still be heard chugging back and forth,
while its signal bell clangs and its pilot screams curses at the boat, the
river and anything else that catches his eye.

It's a chilling story, not for any portents of doom that it might
contain, or even for any fate that the ship's crew and passengers may
have suffered — one presumes that they simply dropped anchor on
the shore and found their own way home. But as much as any of the

state's watery ghost stories, there is something inherent in the tale that offers up a marrow-chilling resonance that is far greater than any lone spirit or tragedy. The image of that vast and glorious vessel, lit up with all the revelry and pageantry that was the paddle steamers' birthright, shunting frustrated passengers back and forth in an ever narrowing, ever more shallow strip of water, is more terrible than anything else Old Muddy can throw at us — and that includes the ghostly fife, flute and drum band that haunts the Pearl River, for example, remembering how they hurled themselves to a watery grave rather than fall into the hands of some pursuing Native Americans.

But it reminds us once again that the river cannot be messed with, because it will exact a price if it is. And if the river don't getcha, the weather probably will.

TRACK THIRTEEN

"Sneaking Sally through the Alley" by Robert Palmer
from the LP *Sneaking Sally through The Alley* (Island Records)
1974

A recent contributor to that most valued of modern-day Internet communities, Twitter, declared that Louisiana "is a genetic freak show." He, she or it was referring to what political correctness now insists we describe as a cultural melting pot, although it should also be pointed out that the state in general possesses more indigenous racial minorities than all of the rest put together, many of whom could be ascribed to a simple freak of reproductive nature — mommy was a Creole Princess, daddy was a hexadecaroon.

The mathematical precision with which Louisiana law and custom could appraise and label an individual's racial background would astonish, and probably horrify, 21st-century America, especially after a similar system was subpoenaed by Nazi Germany in order to quantify Jews.

First there was the mulatto, a person with one white parent and one black. Then came the quadroon, a person of one-quarter black ancestry and three-quarters Caucasian ancestry — that is, one white parent and one biracial. The octoroon is a person of fourth-generation black ancestry: one black grandparent and seven white. A hexadecaroon has one white parent and one octoroon; and so, doubtless, on.

The old vaults in St Louis cemetery, New Orleans.

We would never even think of making such distinctions today. We live, after all, in an age when a person's ethnicity is rarely referred to, not even when posting a police "wanted" description. Be on the lookout, we are told, for a tall man in a dark green anorak, because we all know that criminals never change their clothes.

It could well be to avoid that self-same confusion that . . . officially, anyway . . . 19th- and early-20th-century Louisiana derived such a great deal of comfort from having so precise a system for identifying the makeup of its inhabitants. If you knew you were on the lookout for a mulatto with murder in his eyes, then you wouldn't go wasting police time by reporting any homicidal hexadecaroons whom you might also have spotted on your travels.

Prior to that, such differentiations were tied in with the slave trade, and it was a controversial system even then, particularly the farther north one traveled: in 1859, for example, a new play opened in New York City, the Anglo-Irish playwright Dion Boucicault's *The Octoroon*. It raised eyebrows from the outset — set in Louisiana, with its cast of slaves and slave-owners, *The Octoroon* was viewed either as passionately abolitionist, which set one section of the populace against it, or fiercely pro-slavery, which enflamed the other half.

The author himself simply insisted (in a letter to the governor of Louisiana) that it was "a picture of plantation life, not the less faithful because drawn by one who feels so warmly towards the sunny South"; he defended himself against both sides of the political divide by declaring, "I am a Democrat, and a Southern Democrat, but do not mix myself up with politics in any way." His play was neither commentary nor condemnation. It was a fond observation.

Still, he was forced to withdraw it from the New York stage (it traveled to New Orleans instead). He would smart for many years on the outrage he felt when he discovered that many of his foes had not even seen the play. They had simply looked at its title and read their own interpretations into that; when the Civil War erupted the following year, Boucicault's little play could (and was) even numbered among the myriad sparks that ignited the conflagration.

The term "octoroon," and its manifold brethren too, remained loaded in political and civil rights circles. As the 19th century progressed, however, it took on another resonance, one that was first fanned and then rendered famous by the vice trade — and not only in Louisiana.

Los Angeles once boasted an octoroon brothel, where Madame Bolanger promised "you will receive enough sport to last for a year to come." Others flourished in other cities. But the best known of them all was Mahogany Hall in New Orleans, where Lulu White — the self-styled Diamond Queen of the Demi-Monde — provided an exclusively octoroon service for an equally exclusively all-white clientele. Other establishments and their clientele favored young Creole girls, prompting many of the better families to send their daughters away to the strictest Catholic schools, rather than risk them falling prey to the bordello life.

But, of course, such precautions could never end the trade, and,

One of New Orleans photographer E.J. Bellocq's good-time gals.

once the city's passions had been set ablaze, those flames would never be quelled. Why else would Englishman Robert Palmer have gone there to sing a song about walking a prostitute home?

"Well, that's one interpretation," he laughed when I asked him. "Although it could have been more innocent than that." But then he laughed. "But what the hell? It does sound like that, doesn't it?"

Sneakin' Sally through the Alley, Robert Palmer's first solo album, from 1974, stands among New Orleans–based producer and legend Allen Toussaint's greatest achievements, at least among the white acts with whom he worked. Best known, at that time, as vocalist with the British-based, Humble Pie–like rock/R & B act Vinegar Joe, immediately after that band's split, Palmer decamped to Toussaint and partner Marshall Sehorn's Sea Saint Studios with just one musical intention.

"I wanted to make a record that didn't sound like anything else," Palmer recalled in the mid-1980s — by which time, unfortunately, *most* of his records sounded like everybody else's. In the arms of Toussaint and the Sea Saint house band the Meters, however, that was never to be a concern. "I was a big Little Feat fan, and that was always going to be an influence, but I'm English, so anything that I took from them, I fed through my own background. And what came out was a sound that was neither one thing nor another."

Or, as Toussaint put it to writer Eric Olsen, "In New Orleans, the music isn't just in the clubs or on the dance floor, it's in everything. You can feel it in the street, see it in the buildings, taste it in the food. The syncopation and the strut of the second line brass bands [those that follow the main musicians at carnivals etc.], the frenzied intensity of the Mardi Gras Indian chants, and the driving rhythms of blues, jazz and R & B are as essential to this city as eating and sleeping."

They were essential to Palmer as well. Sea Saint Studios, Palmer told *Playboy* in 1977, provided him with "the perfect environment with an unforced instrumental focus." The arrival at the studio of

Little Feat's Lowell George, meanwhile, offered him "a catalytic relationship aimed at no more than making expressive music. No sugary attention to precision, no raucous volume." The result was an often lazy, sometimes louche, but never less than aurally captivating slow-shoe shuffle through the swamp, an album whose songs bleed into and through one another with almost psilocybic ease.

At a time when even the best rock critics were describing the Doobie Brothers as the epitome of "laid back," and championing their harmonic tribute to the Mississippi River, "Black Water," as the epitome of what the swamp was all about, *Sneakin' Sally through the Alley* was reclining on a rocker on the porch, watching the world through a gap-toothed grin and not even stirring to brush the flies from its eyes. Occasionally it might swig from a bottle of firewater, or strum a few chords on a battered acoustic guitar. But then again, it might not. It was that relaxed, and it was that content, because inside the creative bubble that the team formed around them, music was not made, it was grown — tendrils of sound that snake out from the rhythm base to enfold and enrapture anything that passes by.

A lot like the girls it *may* have been written about.

The Queens of Storyville were the madams who ran the brothels and bordellos, many of whom have in turn become as famous as the establishments they operated. A local publication called *The Blue Book* was dedicated to detailing the pleasures of Storyville, and it overflows with its own tales of the women who ruled the streets. There was Hilma Burt, who ran bordellos on Basin Street and Iberville Street, and who was recommended to her visitors as being "of a type that pleases most men of today — the witty, pretty and natty — a lady of fashion. Her managerial possibilities are phenomenal to say the least, and . . . there are no words for her ladies — one can only realize the grandeur of feminine beauty and artistic settings after an hour or so in the palace of Helma [sic] Burt."

There was the Countess Willie V. Piazza, whose girls were described as "the most handsome and intelligent Octoroons in the

United States. You should see them; they are all cultivated entertainers." A society lady whose taste in fashion influenced half the city, the countess (a title she borrowed, rather than deserved) also enjoyed some remarkable friends; it was in the parlor of her North Basin Street establishment that the Honduran Revolution of 1910 was planned.

There was Lulu White, a West Indian immigrant whose sumptuous life and times provided the inspiration for Mae West's character in the movie *Belle of the Nineties*; and Floro Randella, of whom the *Blue Book* (which was, in fact, produced from an office at White's Mahogoney Hall establishment) enthused, "better known as Snooks, the Italian beauty, [she] is one woman among the fair sex who is regarded as an all-around jolly good fellow. Nothing is too good for Snooks, and she regards the word Fun as it should be, and not as a money-making word. She is a good fellow to all who come in contact with her."

There were so many of them, but all had one thing in common. Until 1917 saw their trade swept away, they were New Orleans' number one tourist attraction.

The Queens of Storyville — 10 Notorious New Orleans Madams

Countess Willie V. Piazza

Emma Johnson

Floro Randella

Hattie C. Hamilton

Hilma Bert

Josie Arlington

Kate Townsend

Lulu White

Mamie Hines

Marianne LeSoleil Levant

I'll do it for twenty cents, hot papa. I can't dance with no dry throat.

In 1940, folklorist Lyle Saxon spent a night in the company of the Zulus, one of the myriad tribes that came together each year to celebrate Mardi Gras in New Orleans, and one whose reputation for licentiousness, sex and abandon ensured that a few hours in their company was never going to be dull. "She did a little kicking step," Saxon reported, "raised her dress and showed her linen."

"Linen" in 1940 had a very different connotation to how it sounds today.

New Orleans and sex may not be synonymous, at least not in the way that Times Square and sex, or Soho and sex, once were. But the city has its notoriety regardless, which popular history focuses on the Storyville red-light district, which entered the 20th century as the only legal source of prostitutes in the entire United States, and where establishments like the Mahogany Club catered to every sexual taste. But even that was little more than a pale shadow of what had once existed here, a century previous when the city's most sordid underbelly was flavored by a far more appropriately named den of vice — the Swamp.

It wasn't a huge place, the Swamp, but it was part of a long-held tradition. Go back to the days when Louisiana itself was a foul-smelling, swamp-ridden and bug-infested wasteland, into which the French settlers had imposed a handful of hardy communities, and New Orleans might well have been populated wholly by whores and their customers — or so one of the city's first governors believed. Asking one of his priests how best to raise the city's moral standard, he was told to send away all the disreputable women. "But then there will be no women left here at all," the governor replied.

Neither was he exaggerating. The very first settlers dispatched to Nouvelle Orleans from France, by King Louis XIV in 1721, were convicts — 88 luckless transportees, of whom 27 were women, primarily petty criminals and prostitutes. Of course they continued to ply their trade once they reached the settlement, because what else could they

do? The only work in the region was distinctly masculine stuff —
building houses, draining swamps, fighting off wildlife — but a
single woman needed to eat as well.

So they gave the men something to look forward to at the end of
the day, and they continued to do so even after the first boatloads of
more respectable women began to arrive in the city: Ursuline nuns in
1727, and in 1728 French and Canadian orphans . . . "casket girls," as
the locals called them, from the peculiar shape of their luggage.
Soldiers and settlers who married these casket girls were rewarded
with a cow, a rifle and a plot of land.

It's very strange, though. Author and historian Herbert Asbury,
one of the boldest chroniclers of the city's darker side, raises a wry
smile when he points out that, while many of New Orleans' most
established families can trace their lineage back to these newly
arrived ladies of quality, few *if any* of them acknowledge that their
founding matriarch was a hooker.

The Swamp stepped out of the swamps, then, and it found its
home down near the bottom of Girod Street, out where the
Louisiana Superdome now lurks, with its own brutal memories of a
time when the laws of "normal" society were suspended, in the pan-
icked aftermath of Hurricane Katrina. Long before that, in 1957, the
remains of a deconsecrated (and already emptied) cemetery were
cleared to make way for the sports stadium, and the locals said that
the ground was cursed from the moment the first earthmover went
into action. But it was scarcely a happy place even before that.

The Swamp, once again, was aptly named. Poorly drained, and
stinking still, it was no more than an accumulation of shabby
wooden hovels, clustered together for just one purpose, to cater to
the needs of the rivermen and sailors who were washed with every
tide into the city's streets, and who in turn needed to wash the cares
of their livelihoods away. Brothels and bars, taverns and flophouses,
gambling dens and boxing rings, if there was a law against something, it was a virtue in the Swamp, and we must pause here and

wonder why it is that the pastimes that people seem to find the most pleasurable are the ones that the authorities crack down on the hardest.

You want to pay (or be paid) for sex, while flushing your earnings away on a bet, and filling your bladder with the cheapest crap imaginable? *Go right ahead.* Seriously, doesn't government have far more pressing things to worry about than what you do with your spare time and money?

Apparently not, but the Swamp seems to have slithered beneath its attention. The act of actually selling sex for money was not considered a crime in early America; it was the activities that went hand in hand with the exchange — the lewdness, the violence, the harassment, the sheer disruption to "respectable" life in general — that aroused the law's ire. At the same time, though, the Swamp developed such a lawless reputation that it is said, and probably not without some accuracy, that the authorities were simply too scared to go in there because they knew they wouldn't come out again. According to some estimates, for one 20-year moment around the end of the 18th century, there was at least one murder every day in the Swamp, and likely not more than a handful of arrests because, seriously, the police never set foot in there.

Other cities had their equivalent neighborhoods — watch *Gangs of New York* or read some Charles Dickens, and you'll get a glimpse into the kind of lives that were lived out in the Swamp, transferred to New York and London.

You want to run a brothel or a gambling den? Throw up a few boards at the back of the room to act as makeshift cubicles. Screen off the entrance to allow a little privacy. Done. You want to run a hotel? Find yourself a shack with an attic, lay out some blankets and a mattress or two. Done. You want to open a bar? Take a plank and two barrels, one at each end, and make sure you've got enough cheap hooch on hand to stop anybody leaving until you have to throw them out. With the emphasis on cheap. According to Herbert

Asbury, you could get drunk, laid and a good night's sleep for as little as six cents in the Swamp — or about half of the cost of the bucket you just threw up in.

New Orleans — The Cost of Living, Circa 1800

Bucket 12¢
Buttons 5¢ per gross
Candles 10¢ per pound
Cartridge Belts 18¢ - up
Cheese 11¢ per pound
Cigarettes $2.00 for 500
Cigars 1¢ each
Coffee 15¢ per pound
Eyeglasses 10¢ - up
Fishing Rods 9¢ - up
Flour 2¢ per pound
Lady's Dresses 37¢ - up
Lady's Hats 19¢ - up
Lady's Shoes 60¢ - up
Lantern 40¢ - up
Man's Boots 85¢ - up
Man's Coat $1.50 - up
Man's Shoes $1.25 - up
Man's Suit - $2.98 - up
Matches 1¢ per 100
Overalls 35¢
Paint 65¢ per gallon
Pickles 10¢ per pint
Pistol Holsters 15¢ - up
Pocket Knives $1.00
Pocket Watches 98¢ - up
Soap 3¢ per bar
Syrup 40¢ per gallon
Tea 12¢ per pound

The Swamp flourished for as long as it needed to, and a lot of people lived and died there, including many who had no business doing either. But that creeping malaise that we now call progress always finds a way in the end, and by the 1830s or so, a new region had arisen to spearhead the city's tastes in debauchery: Gallatin Street in the old French Quarter.

A short alley that ran from the French Market to the Mint, between North Peters and Decatur Streets, Gallatin Street was lost to redevelopment during the 1930s, a century after its high-water mark. At its peak, however, it was said that you could find anything you wanted in one of its shacks, including whores of every color and country, and every persuasion as well. It was not a place for the faint of heart.

No matter. By 1850, New Orleans was more or less the vice capital of America, the Babylon of the South, with the vice trade running second only to the port as the most profitable business in town. It may or may not be true that, in certain parts of the city, three-fifths of the homes were operating as brothels, but one thing is for certain. By the mid-1880s, travelers were coming from miles away to sample the New Orleans nightlife, and, in 1884, they were going to start arriving from even farther afield. Gallatin Street had spread far beyond its original confines by now, to envelop ever greater swaths of the city. New Orleans was selected to host the 1884 World's Industrial and Cotton Centennial Exposition, a gathering of the great producers from all over the American South and beyond.

The expo was organized, initially, to celebrate the 100th anniversary of the first shipment of cotton from the United States to England, and exhibitors from Mexico, Honduras, Jamaica, British Honduras, Venezuela, Brazil and Guatemala were all on hand. However, the event quickly took on a secondary purpose: to broadcast the city's commercial revitalization following the end of the Reconstruction era, which really should have called for everyone to be on his or her best behavior.

Instead, this is what the city's illustrious guests were forced to witness, as they stepped out of the exhibition grounds. Quoted in the 1938 edition of the *New Orleans City Guide*, an outraged observer tells us this:

Clearly a well traveled young lady, as captured by E.J. Bellocq.

Brilliantly lighted by a new electric flare system, the street is thronged with men of all classes, who enter or emerge from its many saloons and gambling houses, which throb with the raucous sounds of pleasure-bent men and women. Timid crowds of men stand upon the curbstone to catch a glimpse of female limbs draped in gauze of pink and blue. . . .

Arrayed in scant garments, but gorgeous in combinations of color, are young and middle-aged; youthful and fresh, together with wearied and worn, whited sepulchers; watching among the throng which enters, those whom their judgment dictates have money to spend or throw away upon them in remuneration for a display of their utter unconsciousness of virtue.

Can you even begin to imagine the self-righteous huffing and puffing that would be aroused were such a report to be published today? Maybe not. But you can certainly picture the red-faced city fathers gathering in grim consultation to create the most half-assed legislation they could, beneath the now time-honored motto of "something must be done." "Well, this is something. Let's do it."

The authorities didn't think in those terms back then. Or, rather, some of them did. But others were genuinely devoted to making things better for their constituents, and making things work not by throwing money or a think tank full of consultants at them, but by actually addressing the problem at its source. And the problem was — what to do with all the whores?

Easy.

Twenty blocks of prime city real estate, just a little northwest of the French Quarter, were turned over to the New Orleans sex-for-hire trade, framed by the south side of Customhouse Street, from Basin to Robertson Streets, the east side of Robertson Street from Customhouse to St. Louis Streets, and the south side of St. Louis from Robertson to Basin.

The cautiously worded provisions of City Ordinance 13,032 protected the rest of the city from the temptations and evils (and declining property values) of vice by consolidating every imaginable sin into this one single area. Step out of the bounds of Storyville and the full weight of the law would come down upon anybody even vaguely suspected of plying a trade in prostitution. But within, anything and everything were apparently permissible.

Storyville took its name from Alderman Sidney Story, for it was he who pushed through the ordinance in 1897 — that is, 13 years after the Expo, by which time matters had only grown worse. At first, the area he delineated was known as nothing fancier than the District, but local wags and satirists were quick to name it for its creator, and, though poor Sidney would remain mortified for the remainder of his life by his claim to immortality, he was immortal all the same. At one point, Storyville was estimated to be worth a million dollars a month to the whores and madams, sportsmen and gamblers, businessmen and barkeeps, and all the other thousands of trades that flourished beneath its red lights, and while we have few concrete records of the names of the people who lived in the district, we do have their faces. Some of them, anyway.

Compared to either the Swamp or Gallatin Street, Storyville has adopted a luminescence that completely outstrips its sordid reality. The area looms large, for example, in any discussion of American music; it was, after all, the birthplace of jazz. Here it was that the first musicians came together to play what would become that most quintessential of American musical forms, as a permanent sound-track to the bars and bordellos; here it was that successive future generations, the young Satchmo (Armstrong's nickname meant a coal delivery boy) included, either descended or were raised, to learn the music firsthand but, more importantly, to absorb the culture. Jazz, no matter how cosmopolitan it may quickly have become, was as indigenous to Storyville as any of the sounds being strummed in the swamps beyond, just as Storyville itself was unique to New Orleans.

Perhaps that is what attracted Ernest J. Bellocq to its side, just as Bellocq today has attracted so many other artists to his name. Two books rattle on the back seat of our rental car; a slim volume of poetry by Natasha Trethewey, *Bellocq's Ophelia*, and *Bellocq's Women* by Englishman Peter Everett. Both evoke an age for which we can only wax nostalgic; both find a beauty in a life we're encouraged to be disgusted by; both find romanticism in the work of this funny little man.

Ernest J. Bellocq was a professional photographer, a Creole from the French Quarter who set up a business as a commercial photographer and drew his clientele primarily from the many shipping companies that were based in town. Ships and machinery were his specialty and, once a year, the same flurry of Mardi Gras carnival floats and scenes that occupied every other local photographer of the day. It seems to have been a profitable operation, but scarcely

An orderly, early 20th-century view of Metairie Cemetery.

one that would mark him out as anything other than a jobbing photographer. Around 1912, however, and now in his late thirties, Bellocq started taking the photographs for which he is cherished and remembered today.

Touring Storyville with his camera, he began photographing the girls who worked there. There could be, and probably were, any number of reasons why he did this. It has been suggested that it was a commercial assignment, the girls themselves hiring him to take their pictures so that they might be used to further their careers — a keepsake for a favorite customer, an advertisement for their service, or even a job application. As in every other walk of life, there was a distinct social hierarchy that existed among the brothels, from the lowest of the low, which catered to the rough ends of a port town's populace, to the high-class cathouses where the politicians and businessmen turned out. Few girls could have been content remaining at the lowest scale; a photograph (and a few enthusiastically declared letters of reference) might well have helped them begin climbing up the scale.

"There are indeed all sorts of men who visit here," begins one of Tretheway's beautiful stanzas. "And then there are those, of course, whose desires I cannot commit to paper," it ends. The recommendations of one of those customers would have gone a long way in the annals of the trade.

Or maybe Bellocq simply enjoyed photographing the girls. He would not have been alone in that, after all; among the many artistic treasures produced in 20th-century France, there exists a cache of erotic photographs created by a gentleman whom posterity has named Monsieur X. According to French writer Alexandre Dupuoy, who cataloged the collection following its sale to a Parisian book-seller in the mid-1970s, Mr. X pursued his photographic interests exclusively in the Parisian brothels, where the girls would be paid their usual going rate simply to pose for his camera.

Occasionally, Mr. X would be accompanied by a male friend, but neither man took part in the action that followed. The girls — whose names were frequently noted on the backs of the photographs . . . FanFan, Gypsi, Nénette, Suzy and so on — were the sum of Mr. X's interest. "Nude or scantily clad, in either academic or very licentious poses. There are no men" beyond the odd occasion when Mr. X's companion strayed into camera shot or, once, when the photographer himself is caught in a mirror's reflection.

His subjects appreciated his visits. "What's nice is that with Mr. X, we never have to do any of the oddish stuff we sometimes have to do with some of the others," wrote one of his subjects in her diary. "All he wants is to take pictures of us. Marie, Fanfan and I think maybe he's impotent, and it makes us laugh, but never in a mean way."

Maybe Bellocq was the same, taking a satisfaction that we simply cannot imagine (or we can, but are too polite to speak it aloud) from watching the girls as they arranged themselves thoughtfully, clicking his shutter while they watched the birdie, and then developing his handiwork once he got back to his home. Maybe.

Whatever Bellocq's intentions, however, he created a storehouse

The old St Louis cemetery, early in the last century.

of imagery that remains one of the most captivating of its age, as Susan Sontag reflected following the rediscovery of his raison d'être in a New Orleans junk shop in the late 1960s: "The pictures are unforgettable — photography's ultimate standard of value. And it's not hard to see why the trove of glass negatives by a hitherto unknown photographer working in New Orleans in the early years of this century became one of the most admired recoveries in photography's widening, ever incomplete history."

Bellocq's photographs remain the visual accompaniment to any exploration of Storyville. The beauty of his subjects is both physical and spiritual, and, although many of the photographs are clearly erotic, it is so much easier to imagine the young women simply posing for the joy of doing so than with any of the predatory (or otherwise) intent with which prostitutes are traditionally displayed.

A tousle-haired beauty smiles and exhibits her puppy; another scratches a butterfly into the wall plaster of her room; a third smiles from beneath a mass of curls, perched naked on the windowsill of a crib, a tiny room that rented by the hour. One poses in her Sunday-best hat and coat, while her roommate slumbers on the bottom deck of their bunk bed. One strikes a careless stance with a glass of Raleigh Rye, while her vertically striped tights disappear beneath a loosely draped shawl.

Some of the girls pose naked, some could be off to church. Some smile coquettishly, some look positively pained. Some are beautiful, some look wretched. Some show signs of censorship — following Bellocq's death, it seems, a God-fearing relative made an attempt to at least render the photographer's subjects unrecognizable. Others could still do a girlie magazine proud. There's no order or organization to the photos that Bellocq took. But they offer us a glimpse not only into a long lost world, but into some of its secrets as well.

And yet . . . and yet. Although Storyville might well be the best-known red-light district in American history, it did not house the best-known brothel in New Orleans. Such names as Mamie Hines, who operated a bordello at 1301 Bienville, or Hilma Bert's, whose Mirror Ballroom on Basin Street gave Jelly Roll Morton his first paying gig, have passed into legend. But not one of them is as well known, or as universally recognized, as the House of the Rising Sun.

TRACK FOURTEEN

"The House of the Rising Sun" by the Animals
single (EMI)
1964

It seems churlish to point this out so early, but there's some doubt as to whether the House of the Rising Sun ever existed. There are a few places that have claimed to be the original, but if you actually follow the lyric, we're not even certain what the house was. It might have been a bordello. But it could as easily have been a jailhouse, a hospital, a tavern, a plantation house or even a slave pen. We just assume, and then we purvey the historical record in search of something to back our assumptions up.

In the early 1820s, a Rising Sun Hotel stood on Conti Street, in the French Quarter, before being destroyed by fire in 1822. The site was excavated archaeologically in 2005, and the diggers not only discovered a vast quantity of rouge and cosmetics, there was also an advertisement whose language was a masterpiece of euphemism for anybody seeking a good-time girl.

Another Rising Sun grew up on the riverfront in the Carrollton neighborhood towards the end of that same century, a social club that appears to have been above suspicion, but that wasn't saying much in an age where corruption was officialdom's middle name.

A third flourished between 1862 and 1874 at 1614 Esplanade

Avenue, and this one was purportedly titled for the woman who ran it, a Madam Marianne LeSoleil Levant, whose name itself means "rising sun." A fourth, for which some sources confusingly relate the same story, was placed by the guidebook *Offbeat New Orleans* at 826–830 St. Louis Street, where archaeologists did uncover the remains of a brothel on this very site in 2005.

A fifth, more modern construction that was named for, rather than as, the original establishment can be found at 333 Bourbon Street. There's a House of the Rising Sun B and B in Historic Algiers Point, across the Mississippi River from the French Quarter. And there's probably a whole bunch more. It's a little like traveling up and down the American East Coast in that, wherever you go, George Washington spent the night there, and, if he didn't, then Paul Revere did. One can only imagine what would have happened had they both demanded a bed the same night.

So yes, the House of the Rising Sun could have stood upon almost any of these sites. Or it may not have stood on any of them, and it might not have existed at all.

No matter. For it came to life anyway.

The earliest recorded version of the song called "The House of the Rising Sun" was made around 1933 by the one-eyed Appalachian fiddler Clarence "Tom" Ashley and singer Gwen Foster. Ashley was almost 40 at the time he cut the record. He was born in Bristol, Tennessee, but raised in Shouns, a crossroads near Mountain City, Tennessee, where his grandfather ran a boarding house. It was his grandfather who bought eight-year-old Tom his first banjo, while his extended family of aunts and uncles, together with the boarding house's guests (lumberjacks and railroad workers mostly), all taught him songs to play on it.

In 1911, when he was 16, Tom joined a medicine show that was passing through Mountain City. Later he performed at the coal camps and rayon mills in the area, plowing his way through the prodigious quantity of folk songs and ballads that would serve him for much of his career, and which would also be immortalized when he began his recording career, in 1928 for the Gennett Records label. Such now familiar standards as "Haunted Road Blues," "The House Carpenter," "Corrina, Corrina," "Greenback Dollar," "Dark Holler," "The Rude and Rambling Man," the murder ballads "Naomi Wise" and "John Hardy," were all in his repertoire, together with a song that he learned from his grandfather, about a house in New Orleans.

Yet "The House of the Rising Sun" was not unique to Tom Ashley, as folklorist Alan Lomax discovered when he and his father, in their role as curators of the Archive of American Folk Song, commenced their travels around the country (and eventually much of the globe) in search of music.

In Pineville, eastern Kentucky, in September 1937, Lomax and his wife Elizabeth heard (and recorded) the song being sung by one Tilman Cadle. Later that month in Middlesboro, Kentucky, they taped another performance by 16-year-old Georgia Turner, the daughter of a local miner, and were so impressed by her rendering that, four years later, in his songbook *Our Singing Country*, Lomax credited Turner with having written the lyric in the first place. The fact that she would have been just 12 years old when Ashley first recorded it clearly escaped his notice.

Other versions by fellow eastern Kentuckians Bert Martin and Daw Henson followed, but by that time, the first commercially successful recording had been made by Roy Acuff — who probably learned it from Tom Ashley, with whom he occasionally performed. And now the floodgates of appreciation opened. Woody Guthrie, Josh White, Lead Belly, Pete Seeger and the Weavers, Glenn Yarbrough, Frankie Laine, Joan Baez, Miriam Makeba . . . and in 1960, folk singer Dave Van Ronk was about to record his own version of the song, which he learned from a Texan named Hally Wood (who himself picked the song up from the Georgia Turner recording) when a new gun in town, Bob Dylan, beat him to the punch, and tapped it for his debut album.

*The essential version of
one of New Orleans'
most defining songs.*

In the space of less than 30 years, "The House of the Rising Sun" had traveled from the most obscure beginnings that any folk song could have to the mouthpiece of a generation, and it really doesn't matter that Dylan's version is scarcely the most exciting song on his first LP. The mere fact that he recorded it in the first place ensured an entire new audience would soon be singing it.

The song crossed the ocean. One night in 1964, English singer Eric Burdon was visiting a nightclub in his hometown of Newcastle when he heard folkie Johnny Handle perform "The House of the Rising Sun." Burdon's band, the Animals, had just signed their first record deal, with producer Mickie Most; their debut single, "Baby Let Me Take You Home," was in the shops, and they were about to begin their first nationwide tour, supporting the visiting Chuck Berry. It was the perfect opportunity, the band members agreed, to show the rest of the country exactly what they were made of, by developing a live show and a repertoire that stepped far beyond the regulation R & B shuffle that every group of the era seemed doomed to re-create.

Burdon took the news of his discovery into the band's next rehearsal; not the song itself, which they all already knew from Dylan's nasal passage through the lament, but the possibility that it might be withdrawn from the master's grasp altogether and presented as something else.

Guitarist Hilton Valentine, who was charged with rearranging the song for the Animals' disposal, readily acknowledged that it was Dylan who inspired him to the foundation for his endeavors. But it would be another year before producer John Hammond "electrified" Dylan's version of the song, as a (failed and, for many decades, unreleased) experiment in folk rock basics, and *he* took the Animals' rendition as his starting point. Because, whereas Dylan simply strummed the chords, Valentine laced the song with haunted arpeggios, repeating and recurring signatures that layered the song with the dense, hypnotic feel that would allow the performance to go on forever — which, in those days of the three-minute single, it did. Close to five minutes elapsed between beginning and end, a hitherto unheard of length for a simple 45.

But it was not the song's length that most perturbed its makers as they readied it for release. It was its subject matter. At a time when rock 'n' roll was still obsessed with holding hands and undying love, when angst meant not receiving a love letter, and getting out of high school was the sum of most kids' ambition, "The House of the Rising Sun" stood out like a beacon of gross indecency.

Dylan did not fear such improprieties — he even retained the song's feminine point of view when he sang, to ensure that its message was not diluted by commercialism. But Animals drummer John Steel knew that wouldn't fly on 45. "To make it a record or to get across to anybody at the time, you couldn't go singing about a bloody brothel, not to an audience of kids, mothers, whatever. It was the way of the time."

A few deft lyric changes switched the emphasis of the lyric from a bordello to a gambling den, and the gender of the singer from female to male. But there was no diminution of the song's power or meaning. It remained a whore's lament.

"The beauty of that song," Mickie Most explained in 1994, "was that a lot of people already knew it because of the Dylan version, but his version was a drag, it was just him playing his guitar and singing the words. There was no intent or emotion in his voice, he could have been singing his laundry list, which was a problem with a lot of early Dylan, I thought.

"Eric [Burdon] put himself into the song, and it didn't matter that nobody outside Newcastle had really heard of him or the

Animals at that time. They heard Eric's voice and they knew he wasn't messing them around. His mother *was* a tailor, his father *was* a gambler, and every word he sang was gospel truth autobiography. There wasn't another singer in the world who could have put that much soul into that song, and that's what made the record so great for me. A lot of people talk about Alan [Price]'s organ part, or Hilton's guitar, but they would have been meaningless if Eric hadn't put so much feeling into the lyrics."

Recorded in a single take on May 18, 1964, "The House of the Rising Sun" became a monster hit regardless of its unwieldy dimensions, crashing to the top of the U.K. chart that summer of 1964; it repeated that feat in the United States and established the Animals as superstars in both countries. More than that, though, the performance not only ascended to, but remains, one of the mere handful of unquestioned inclusions in any poll of the greatest records of all time.

Dylan himself claimed that the first time he heard the Animals' version of the song that he'd made re-famous, he was so excited that he jumped out of his car, simply because he loved it so much; he also stopped including the song in his live set, after one too many fans came up to ask him why he was covering the band.

Critic Dave Marsh is only one of the many who have proclaimed "The House of the Rising Sun" as the first ever true "folk-rock hit," a record that sounded as though "they'd connected the ancient tune to a live wire," and pointed the way forward for an entire generation of future performers.

The Animals also opened the door for "The House of the Rising Sun" to become one of the chest-beating staples of modern rock, although the Detroit-based psychedelic rock band Frijid Pink cut the only other serious hit version, when they gave it another bite at the Top 10 in 1970. And, from there, we can travel to the disparate energies of performers as far removed as Herbie Mann and Mountain, Nina Simone and John Otway.

But Sinead O'Connor cut the loveliest version, an *a cappella* lament that only slowly intrigues itself into a barrage of broken blues — close your eyes, and you can imagine it wafting out of a crib in Storyville; open them, and you can see the woman singing it, staring to the sky and wishing she was anywhere but there. And so "The House of the Rising Sun" emerges among the most frequently recorded folk songs in the language, and one of the most evocative as well. Ask anybody who has spent his or her own nights of figurative sin and misery within the confines of those storied walls.

"The Carny" by Nick Cave and the Bad Seeds
from the LP *Your Funeral . . . My Trial* (Mute)
1986

The freak show is the greatest of all American traditions.

Other countries had their moments when nature's unfortunates were considered worthy of public exhibition and entertainment — Britain's Elephant Man, for one — but no other nation rejoiced in their exhibition until so late in the day, and none was able to accept these displays into its culture, too, until the image of the carnival barker, rolling 'em up to see the fabulous headless merman, is as much a part of the national psyche as cars with fins and a fridge full of Coca-Cola bottles.

Neither is it considered a graceless profession, even today. True, an especially imaginative confidence trickster might be compared to an especially vociferous carnival barker, and most people know the story today of how Colonel Tom Parker, Elvis' manager, got his start in showbiz on the carnival circuit, placing hot plates under his chickens' feet and charging the people to watch them dance.

But was he more dishonest than any other tradesman whose living depends upon hyping the incredulous? A used car salesman, for example, has chickens of his own, and they'll dance for as long as the test drive lasts. Modern doctors and pharmaceutical salesmen are the direct descendants of the old traveling snake oil salesman, and who's to say that his panaceas and remedies weren't at least as effective as the cure-alls that are being peddled today? Moss, sassafras, orange leaves, chamomile, potato leaves — all of these things had their place in the Louisiana medicine cabinet. River weed was a universal cure-all that the boatmen never grew tired of; crushed crab and crayfish eyes were a certain remedy for several debilitating sicknesses, and if — early in the 20th century — your gas main ever filled with water, you could pump it out and sell it to pet-owners. It was a guaranteed cure for the mange.

Of course there is a certain reluctance among many people today to even refer to the cast of America's traveling circuses as freaks, a politeness that has rendered the term even more redolent of a distant age, a golden age, when America was still the land of wide-open opportunity and cowboys had better things to do than get day jobs and suits, then offer to re-roof your house.

So we call them carnival people instead, and, while that can lead us down some very strange nomenclatural byways of its own (not least of all around Mardi Gras time), it can also take us down some sinister routes as well. The Devil was in league with the carnivals, and many's the town the country over where the circus people were barred from entering, for fear they'd bring Mr. D. down on the doorstep. And he'd be dancing, dancing. . . .

As will gladly be attested by fans of Ray Bradbury, the Midwestern author of *Something Wicked This Way Comes*, the book (but please not the movie) remains the acid test for everyone who says they're not scared of clowns. Just try the ringmaster for size, then.

The carnival came to town only rarely. Once a year, twice if you were lucky. And for weeks beforehand, every kid in the neighborhood would be dreaming of their own piece of the promised magic — to watch, to help, to run away and join. It's the smell of the greasepaint and the roar of the crowd, to be sure. But it's also the freedom, the traveling, the knowledge that, although you usually have a good

Three marvelous views of Lake Pontchartrain, late in the 19th century.

idea of where you'll be spending the next couple of nights, you never know for sure.

Bradbury's own fascination with carnivals was kick-started by . . . a carnival. "During the Labor Day week of 1932" — the same year, coincidentally, that moviemaker Tod Browning unleashed his masterpiece *Freaks* on the American people — "a favorite uncle of mine died; his funeral was held on the Labor Day Saturday. If he hadn't died that week, my life might not have changed because, returning from his funeral at noon on that Saturday, I saw a carnival tent down by Lake Michigan. I knew that down there, by the lake, in his special tent, was a magician named Mr. Electrico."

Mr. Electrico was "a fantastic creator of marvels." Every night, he would be strapped into an electric chair, and, while the audience gazed on in rapt horror, the switch would be flung and he'd fry. And while he fried, while the volts zapped through his body and turned his internal organs into so many smoking husks, he would raise a sword and touch it to the head of every child in the front row, including — on this occasion — the 12-year-old Bradbury. "The electricity rushed down the sword, inside my skull, made my hair stand up and sparks fly out of my ears. He then shouted at me, 'Live forever!' I thought that was a wonderful idea."

The carnival (and its closest relations in the touring concerts and minstrel shows of the Great Depression) was many small towns' closest link with the wider world, and many young townspeople's first contact with it too. And later, though they were familiar with its tricks, they could still be entranced by its magic.

Charles Neville — one of the famous New Orleans Neville Brothers — recalls when he came face to face with the *Rabbit Foot Minstrel Show*, sometime around the early 1950s while still a teenager. It was, the posters outside declared, "The Greatest Colored Show on Earth." But you could probably drop the racial distinction. It was, enthused Neville, just the greatest.

The canvas covered the largest empty space it could find, the cast of almost 30 crowded around the booths and caravans. Add 10 musicians, add the helpers and fixers, and there were almost 50 people riding with the show, each of them charged with something very specific to do. Other professions shoehorned their workers into whatever mean task they were required to do. The carnival sought out your own special talent and then gave you the chance to enact it.

So "there were animals," marveled Neville, and the animal trainers. "Fortune tellers, a strongman, a fat lady, a girl with four legs, Siamese twins, acrobats and . . . a blues tent where a big mama would tell it like it is.

"There were fabulous dancers like Peg Leg Bates and Peg Leg Moffett, who worked miracles on one leg." There were the gay guys "who had the discipline and technique of classical ballet but, for reasons of racism, had been shut out of that world." And there was the jungle show, which opened with an old man sitting on a rock with his cane, and the audience — even those who had seen it all before — wondering what this had to do with the carnival. Even the rhythm of the drums was muted around him, and though they were growing stronger, by imperceptible degrees, he was growing weaker, leaning harder on his stick, his eyes flickering, his breath labored. He would probably be dead before the show was over.

Then a woman appeared dancing to the sudden flurry of a clarinet. She circled around and touched the man — "suggestively," says Neville. "Another female dancer appears. Her dance, punctuated by a trumpet, is more suggestive; she too touches the man." Another dancer, another touch, and with every caress he straightens and strengthens, an old balloon with new life being blown into it, a tired engine being touched with fresh fuel. And suddenly, he is upright, and thrusting into the air, leaping away from the rock where he was slowly dying, to dance the dance of life for the ladies, until it is they who collapse, exhausted, to the ground, while he scans the crowd for fresh conquests. Even a kid knew what the analogy was, and the audience would roar its own understanding. The Jungle Show wasn't a carnival turn. It was the force of life itself.

The *Rabbit Foot Minstrel Show* first stepped out around 1900, under the aegis of its greatest impresario, the white man F. S. Wolcott. It was based in Port Gibson, just outside of Jackson, Mississippi, and a roll call of its featured singers was itself a carnival of the blues — Ma Rainey, Bessie Smith, Louis Jordan, Rufus Thomas, Brownie McGhee, Diamond Teeth Mary. . . . So many of the music's greatest stars found their first feet in the *Rabbit Foot*, and if Wolcott didn't bring his troupe to town, then somebody else sure would. Somebody like *Silas Green from New Orleans*.

Actually, there never was a Silas Green, nor did he hail from New Orleans. Rather, Silas was the strictly fictional creation of vaudeville writer Salem Tutt Whitney, a well-meaning but generally accident-prone chap who wandered around with his buddy Lilas Bean, falling into ever more riotous, if unlikely, scrapes. In 1940, for example, Silas and Lilas found themselves wandering into a hospital with suitcases labeled MD . . . for Mule Driver. Of course they were mistaken for doctors, and, equally inevitably, they wound up in jail.

But, in between times, raved *Time* magazine in its review of the revue, "The show is garnished with such slapstick as putting a patient to sleep by letting him smell an old shoe, such gags as 'Your head sets on one end of your spine and you set on the other.' Silas gets broad at times, but never really dirty. What keeps it moving are its dances and specialty acts, its gold-toothed but good-looking chorus."

In the days before the music halls and movie houses extended their reach into small-town America, and even in the years after that, Silas and Co. offered slapstick to whosoever wanted it. The demand for more was always so great that, for many years, rival carnies happily pitched head-to-head, knowing that the good folk of Wherever's-ville would probably come to see them both.

It was Ephraim Williams, the first African-American circus owner in America, who toured *Silas* around the country, beginning around 1902 and continuing on for the remainder of his life. Then, when Williams died in 1935, his partner Charles Collier simply took up the reins and kept *Silas* going till the mid-1950s, by which time, however, it was part of a dying breed, a race (literally) apart from those that toured the north, but destined to die the same sad death as them. Already buckling beneath the weight of years, there was simply too much competition to keep them alive — too many rival entertainments, too many televisions to keep people at home, too many distractions that seemed new and fresh.

Occasionally, in later years, somebody would step out who remembered the old ways, and could paint their memory high once again. "I knew enough about the old minstrel shows that I used a lot of the shtick they did," Dr. John reminisced of his earliest costumed performances. "My entrance onstage with a puff of smoke was inspired by the minstrel magician. I lifted their snake-handling routine by having one of the dancers, Kalinda, come out dancing with a snake wrapped around her body. . . ." And what he didn't remember, he said, he borrowed "from what I heard from my grand-father and all the other old-timers."

Kalinda also performed a limbo dance beneath a burning bar, "another old spectacle reborn. What I wanted was entertainment for the eyes as well as the ears, and I knew the minstrels were the best there were at laying down a show."

So the carnival was not, as the song insists, over. But it was dying, and, although he was an Australian who had never set foot in the American South, Nick Cave knew enough to record its last breaths, as the Carny himself, the man who led the show and marshaled the freaks, "Dog-boy, Atlas, Mandrake, the Geeks . . . the dwarves. The bird-girl flapping and squawking around" said a silent farewell to a lifestyle that had finally grown too old for this world. And behind him, Cave's band, the Bad Seeds, echoed the convoluted dissonance of the aged showman's grim departure.

Nick Cave is fascinated by the American South in a manner that rarely gets too geographically specific, but whose carapace drapes over locales in your mind's eye regardless.

It peoples his songs, haunts his imagery, informs his music. As early as his first solo album, *From Her to Eternity*, he was covering vintage Presley ("In the Ghetto") and twining the King's mythology with the darker sounds of the Southern psyche, while the title of his sophomore LP, *The Firstborn Is Dead*, reflected the stillborn demise of Elvis' slightly older twin.

The image of the young Presley as an emblematic icon of all the mysteries that the Deep South has to offer is one that Cave has never tired of. He stepped away from Elvis as his career and his compre-hension developed; "Tupelo," from that same second album, was at least partially informed by the 1936 tornado that remains one of the most destructive in American history, while Cave's first novel, *And the Ass Saw the Angel*, conjures up some of the most apocalyptic regional imagery since the days of the dust bowl.

"The Carny" would have felt perfectly at home in its pages.

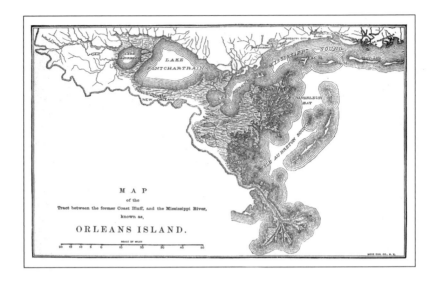

A twisted tale of death and despair, "The Carny" is both a personal lament for a single human being and a keening farewell to a way of life. Guitarist Mick Harvey described the creation of the song. "It's a major, deep work," he told Cave biographer Amy Hanson. Musically, the band echoed a carnival calliope, but one that was galloping both behind and ahead of itself. "There was a template laid out for the song with a click track. What became interesting is that all the sections were different lengths, completely by accident. They were not meant to be, but some of them are 14 bars and some of them are 11, all completely inconsistent. So that meant that all the instrumental passages, the vibraphones and piano interiors, became irregular. The melody had an intentional length, but then there would be an extra bar."

And around that bar, the buzzards flew, picking the flesh off the rain-sodden corpse, conjured up by German-born guitarist Blixa Bargeld after Cave had left the studio one night. "I came back the next day and Blixa had put his guitar on it," Cave told Hanson. "I hadn't really sung on it yet. I just sat in an armchair with all these verses and notes and stuff, and we constructed the music from a very rough perspective. Blixa had come in and done this really beautiful guitar which sounded like a dying horse . . . and he said, 'well the song's about a fucking dying horse, isn't it?'" At the song's climax, the absent Carny's horse, Sorrow, is laid to rest before the circling buzzards.

Like "a bedtime story read by the Devil to stop his children from sleeping," said one critic, "['The Carny' is] an uncomfortable tale which goes nowhere and teaches nothing, but which revels in the sheer unpleasantness of its projected imagery." But it is also pure Louisiana, pure bayou, in essence if not in lyric. It's the same creeping, creaking menace that permeates the best of Creedence or the rest of Dr. John, the jumped-up energy that fired Dave Bartholomew's "The Monkey" and the Spiders' seething "Witchcraft" — songs whose sheer energy testify to the electricity that has always fired the local music scene — and the fact that, standing on the shores of Lake Pontchartrain, you can almost smell the straw of the animal cages, and hear the shriek of the curious. "The Carny" plays to and through all of these things, until its stuttering circularity leaves you breathless with night terrors.

Or it should. Today, you're simply standing on Lakeshore Drive, watching the traffic cross the water on the Pontchartrain Causeway and wondering how this could ever have once been fairground country. Such once-storied and glittering names as Bucktown, West End, Milneburg and Little Woods stood here, while Spanish Fort, the self-styled Coney Island of the South, housed America's first submarine, a rusted crate that was pulled from the lake and was generally (if not conclusively) believed to be the Confederate experiment *Pioneer*, built in New Orleans in the fall of 1861 as the forerunner to a proposed fleet of "Trans-Mississippi Submarines," before being scuttled in the New Basin Canal when the Federal Navy captured the city the following year.

In those days, as far as the eye could see, mile upon mile of prime lakeshore resort property that glistened with amusement parks, dance pavilions, saloons and picnic areas. Little cabins perched on the short wooden piers to offer weekend retreats, jazzmen serenaded away the nights at Tranchinas and the Tokyo Gardens while the boardwalk at Milneburg was a magical playground for the young Joseph Sharkey Bonano . . . a.k.a. trumpeter Sharkey Banana.

Or, before that, this was one of the secret meeting places of the voodoo elite, documented by Lafcadio Hearn with such bold and brilliant flashes of color that there is scarcely a literary reference since then that does not incorporate at least the ghost of his prose. Poised for the duration somewhere "on the lake coast from Spanish Fort to Milneburg," Hearn watched in awe not only as the revelers celebrated a St. John's Eve, June 23, in the early 1890s, but as nature itself joined the party.

Reading like a lyric from a primeval "Who Do You Love," Hearn's prose is so deliciously purple that you could paint aubergines with it.

> *The night was dark and on the eastern sky hung a black cloud, from which now and then burst flashes of lightning which lit up the road, the bayou and the surrounding swamp with a lurid glow. Groups of men and women could be seen standing around blazing pine-knot fires, their dark copper-colored faces weirdly gilded by the red flames and their black forms thus illuminated appearing gigantic and supernatural against the opaque background of the lake and sky on one side, and the mystical darkness just tinged with starlight of the seemingly limitless swamps on the other.*

The Carny would have been at home there as well, the firelight glittering in his beady black eyes, his waxed moustache a grimace across his watching face, his black garb as impressive as the black bodies around him, and all so close to New Orleans that he could have reached out one immaculately gloved hand and extinguished every city light between his thumb and forefinger.

So close, but so far removed as well. Several lifestyles removed the grass of the lakeside from the grit of the city, and the whole thing was more or less obliterated, if not by the storms that took the light structures unawares, then by man, who just churned up everything, the first chance he got.

This entire shoreline was extended by about 2,000 feet into the lake in the late 1920s, a reclamation project that the waters have long since forgiven. On this side of the lake, anyway. Back up a matter of 25 miles, though, retrace your footsteps to revisit Highway 61 and a turning just outside of LaPlace, and you'll hear a very different story.

TRACK
SIXTEEN

"Black Juju" by Alice Cooper
from the LP *Love It to Death* (Warner Bros. Records/Straight)
1971

A little under a century ago, on the southwestern bank of Lake Pontchartrain, there stood three tiny towns named Ruddock, Wagram and Frenier Beach — which wasn't a beach in the slightest, although it would later boast a pier and a bathhouse, and a wooden pavilion where the locals made merry.

We passed here on the way down, as River Road took us through LaPlace, and, for the moment, we thought nothing of it. So we double back to find that junction where Highway 55 North is spit out, turn east on a typically rutted asphalt road, bump across the tracks of the Illinois Central Railroad, and finally we're there, wherever there might be.

Even when the place was booming, that asphalt was a boon yet to come. But it was a thriving community regardless, three towns spaced around four miles apart, and largely peopled by German immigrants who lived by lumber and farming. Throughout the first years of the 20th century, the Burton Lumber Company and the Ruddock Cypress Company were big business in these parts, with the Burtons estimating that there was somewhere in the region of four million linear feet of cypress logs, just laying there for the taking.

So they took them, and the communities around grew — if not rich, then at least reasonably comfortable on the proceeds. Ruddock, Louisiana, was the biggest community and headquarters, of course, of the Ruddock Cypress Company; the town was largely constructed on the lake itself, its one- and two-story houses and offices rising on great stilts from the swamps. Further stilts supported the wooden sidewalks that ran the length of the village, so you could pass from the community center to the blacksmith without even thinking of getting your shoes damp: from the Holy Cross Catholic Church to the railroad depot and even out to the Owl Saloon, a men-only bar which discretion had parked about half a mile south.

Frenier Beach and Wagram were smaller, but no less industrious. Here, the locals specialized in two complementary trades, cabbage farming and barrel stave manufacturing — complementary because the harvested cabbages would then be packed into the locally made barrels for shipment, via the railroads, to the north.

By 1915, much of the property around Frenier Beach was owned by one woman, "Aunt" Julia Brown. A woman of color she may have been, but she was wealthy and wise. She was also a witch, or a voodoo priestess, and few of her neighbors enjoyed passing by her home, particularly if she was out on the porch. Aunt Julia was a songwriter, you see, but the songs that she wrote and sang to herself were scarcely the stuff from which comfortable dreams were woven.

"One day I'm gonna die," she sang, "and I'm gonna take all of you with me." Or sometimes "On the day I die, I'll take Frenier with me." Different tellings conjure up different lyrics, and nobody seems to have bothered writing down the rest of the song. It doesn't matter either way, because she was right. She did.

The Great West Indies Storm hit the United States on September 29, 1915. Modern equipment would allow us to know it was a category three, moving northwest from the Gulf of Mexico at around 14 miles per hour, with sustained winds near its center of 115 miles per hour.

Down in New Orleans, the *Times-Picayune* newspaper had been warning of its approach for a couple of days, although the only way you'd know that would be if somebody aboard one of the passing trains dropped a copy off — Frenier had no newspaper of its own; hell, it didn't even have a grocer's store, so unless you wanted to live on cabbage and whatever you caught in the swamp, you'd have to rely on the railroads for that as well, handing your shopping list and cash to the engineer when the train passed through in the morning, and then collecting your provisions from him when it came back in the afternoon.

So yeah, there was a storm coming, but to be honest, more people were worried about Aunt Julia's song than paid any heed to a bit of wind. *On the day I die, I'll take Frenier with me.* Well, now she was dead, breathing her last on the same day that the storm first hove into view, and today she'd be buried, on a windy Wednesday at the end of the month.

Windy and windier. The lake was storm tossed, and the first trees were already being pulled up by their roots. Railroad maintenance teams were on standby in case any wires came crashing down or trees collapsed onto the track. The first reports were coming in of more serious danger. At Bayou LaBranche, a tiny setup where the Illinois Central could refill their engine boilers, the station had just been washed away, and its occupants had to swim for their lives.

Wagram was under water, the Rigolets Railroad Bridge was washed away, and the storm was bearing down on Frenier Beach. But Frenier Beach had a funeral to attend. Aunt Julia may have unnerved people, but they admired her as well, and the whole town seemed to be pouring out to pay their final respects. The funeral service would begin at four.

But the storm wouldn't wait. The wind was screaming now, and the mourners who gathered around the old lady's coffin were suddenly scattered as the windows of her house blew in, and the walls began to peel away. Then the winds snatched up the coffin and carried it into the bayou, along with everything else it could gather — livestock and the living included. Later, once the winds had died down and the waters were finally agreeing to recede, Aunt Julia's body was found deep within the cypress swamp.

But only her body. Her casket had disappeared, along with more or less everything she had owned . . . the personal possessions that she kept around her house as well as the house itself and most of the property she had collected around Frenier Beach. And the people who lived in Frenier Beach — the ones who were found, at least — were buried in a mass grave in Manchac Swamp. There was a graveyard in Wagram, located on a shell Indian midden, but it was too far to carry the dead through the storm-wracked carnage. So the survivors made rafts from driftwood, and the dead were floated across the lake to their final resting place.

Frenier Beach itself had disappeared. Its remains operated for a time as a lakeside resort, and a subsequent landowner built the pier and a pavilion, but further storms and natural erosion all took their toll on the business. Or so the realists said. The locals, however, had another opinion. They still blamed Aunt Julia.

They still blamed black juju . . . juju being magic, and black being its nature, the darkest magic. A voodoo curse.

That was certainly what the Alice Cooper band was thinking about as they created the song that closes their third album, 1971's *Love It to Death*. And, truthfully, how many other bands had ever even dreamed of raising such demons in a pop song?

"It's not that we threw all the rule books out the window," explained drummer Neal Smith, whose propulsive percussion is the heartbeat of the song. "But we really had an open slate to work with. There were no preconceived notions. But we were honing our theatrics, and what we wanted was a way to kill Alice onstage every night, a song to perform while we did it. By the time we reached our third album, *Love It to Death*, we realized that violence was around us all the time. We never focused on it, but we were thinking we

From 1971, the Alice Cooper band's Love It To Death, *which featured the chilling "Black Juju."*

should have an execution onstage." Nine minutes of drum and basics, "Black Juju" is a primal chant, a silent scream, a lullaby for the sleeping dead, a reminder that bodies need their rest — until it's time to wake up, and the voice that calls for resurrection is one of the eponymous Cooper's most terrifying, in a career that was littered with such horror and gore that it is still possible to ask precisely how five young men with a penchant for live snakes, dead babies and an onstage guillotine ever broke through to win the hearts of two continents.

Legend has it that Alice Cooper's big TV break came when the band was asked to appear in an advertisement for indigestion powder. They played your stomach before you took the cure. But legend doesn't always tell the truth. And sometimes it's better that way.

At the Toronto Peace Festival, Cooper threw a live chicken into the audience. He thought it would fly away ("I mean, they have wings, don't they?"); instead, the audience ripped it to pieces, and, the following day, the watching press swore blind that Alice had bitten off the bird's head and sucked out its blood. "After that we had to check in with the Humane Society every town we played," Cooper said.

But then they released "I'm Eighteen" (they were all closer to 28 at the time, but that didn't seem to matter), the ultimate teen anthem for the newly born 1970s, and suddenly everything fell into place.

When Alice Cooper played London for the first time, headlining over the local master of hellfire and horror, Arthur Brown, the Alice Cooper Band stole the show, hacking up dollies and winding everything up by placing their singer in the electric chair and frying him. Another time, a 20-foot-tall cardboard Alice, naked except for a strategically placed snake, brought London traffic to a halt when the lorry it was on broke down in the middle of Piccadilly Circus. "We act as a mirror" was the group's only explanation for their fame. "People see themselves through us."

Alice Cooper himself was actually Vince Furnier, the son of a Michigan preacher man. Moving to Phoenix, the young Furnier found a band, changed his name and miraculously built a lifestyle around it, first by developing a reputation as the very worst band in Arizona and then by moving to Los Angeles and becoming the worst band in California, revolting and repulsing all who chanced upon them.

By 1971, however, Alice was hotter than hell. They sang of straitjacketed lunatics and pretties for you . . . which weren't pretty at all. They reenacted street fights and executions, and their latest LP came with a pair of black eyes that looked like two fat, dead tarantulas. They took snakes and inflatable sex dolls onstage with them. If something was sacred they would spit on it, if it was holy they'd hack it to pieces. The kids, needless to say, loved every minute of it. As *Life* magazine put it, "Confessing fantasies most people'd rather die than reveal, Alice Cooper became the scapegoat for everybody's guilts and repressions. People project on him, revile him, ridicule him. Some would doubtless like to kill him."

"Black Juju" was the peak of the Cooper band's development. It was released in 1971, but it had little to do with any of the other music percolating around that particular year. . . . Maybe there were a few Brit bands experimenting with odd moods that year — Comus with their acoustic ode to the eponymous Greek God, East of Eden with the oddly sinister "Jig-a-Jig" instrumental, Black Widow demanding that we "Come to the Sabbat" and, of course, anything by Black Sabbath — but they were all strangely English, strangely polite and strangely not really very strange by comparison.

"Black Juju," on the other hand, was everything you've ever dreamed a dark mass could be, without even suggesting that anything was out of the ordinary. The most frightening things are the ones you least suspect.

Bandmate Dennis Dunaway came up with "Black Juju" in the first place — "he didn't get the nickname Dr. Dreary for nothing," says Smith. "He was one of the main creators of 'Dead Babies,' too." At first it was just an idea and a rhythm, pieced together while the Cooper band toured.

"It was worked on in hotel rooms," Smith continues. "We really didn't have a rehearsal studio; our rehearsal studio was the stage, so we sketched it out in hotel rooms on telephone books, and we all agreed it needed a heavy dark African percussion. I wanted to work on the percussion way beyond anything I'd done before. I wanted it to be a big feature drum song, and it was the perfect vehicle. There's a lot of music that uses that tribal primitive vibe, but for me it was like taking Gene Krupa and putting him on floor toms. Gene Krupa in Haiti.

"I was a percussionist. I learned all the rudiments early on and then went into orchestra, so my background was open to everything percussive, and one of my big influences was jungle drums, native American, African, raw percussion."

So he did it.

Performed live for the first time on Midsummer Day 1970 — a coincidence of timing that opens up its own can of neo-pagan wormery — "Black Juju" quickly found its feet. According to Smith, "it was the end of the show, the finale, when we strapped Alice into the electric chair and fried him. And then Alice comes back to life . . ." screaming "wake up" into the faces of the front row, while all around the undead rise in a choking sea of feathers and smoke, and the band drives headlong into madness.

"We'd have the smoke bombs, and Alice was ripping up the feather pillows, and Mike Bruce had some CO_2 canisters and would blast the feathers into the audience, and that was the finale of the show. It was," Smith understates, "very explosive"; as explosive as the storm that smashed into Aunt Julia's house, or the waters that tugged the living to their doom; as explosive as the skeletal fists that punch out of mossy sarcophagi in some dimly remembered horror flick; as explosive as any of the hurricanes that have battered life into submission in the forests of cypress and swamp and whose echoes can still be heard late at night. Echoes that sound like that drumbeat.

TRACK SEVENTEEN

"The Ripper" by Judas Priest
from the LP *Sad Wings of Destiny* (Gull)
1976

The city of Gretna, Louisiana, lies just across the Mississippi from New Orleans' Garden District. The parish seat of Jefferson Parish, it was founded in 1836 and prospered as a halt on no fewer than three railroad lines, the Missouri Pacific, the Texas and Pacific and the Southern Pacific, whose clanging bells and thunderous wheels live on in the Neil Young song of the same name.

It was Mechanicsham back then, a tribute to the townspeople's primary trade; it became Gretna in 1913, and, though it grew, it largely slumbered, a small fish across the water from the leviathan New Orleans. It kept itself apart from the city, too: proud to call its residents its own, rather than allow their birthright to be subsumed into the metropolis across the water. But if Gretna would not go to New Orleans, New Orleans had no hesitation in going to Gretna.

It wasn't always a happy arrangement. In 2005, in the aftermath of Hurricane Katrina, the Gretna police department won widespread condemnation after allegedly setting up roadblocks to prevent the storm's victims from entering their fair city, even threatening them with firearms as they crossed the Crescent City Connection bridge.

Close to a century earlier, however, they would have been very wise to take similar precautions.

Early in the morning of March 10, 1919, grocer's wife Mrs. Charles Cortimiglia awoke to discover her husband locked in unequal combat with a large man in dark clothing. Her husband had just his bare hands with which to defend himself; his assailant had an ax with which he ruthlessly rained blows down upon Charles' defenseless body.

Desperately, Mrs. Cortimiglia grasped the couple's two-year-old daughter in her arms and pleaded with the attacker for mercy. Wordlessly, he replied, bringing the ax down on both of them. The child was killed, Mrs. Cortimiglia received a fractured skull. Then the attacker left as noiselessly as he had come.

The Mad Axman of New Orleans had struck again.

There has, according to most of the guidebooks, never been a shortage of crazies in Louisiana — or any other state in the union, come to think of it. Few, however, have tied their criminal deprecations so thoroughly into an appreciation of music as the Mad Axman of New Orleans, a felon whose reign of terror extended for close to 18 months and which still lurks unsolved in the annals of local misdoings.

The comparisons to London's Jack the Ripper are endless, both in the unsolved pages of Louisiana crime and in the acres of newsprint that have been dedicated to speculation as to his identity and motive. The Ripper killed five (but very likely six) victims in the space of almost three years; New Orleans' Mad Axman was responsible for as many in half that time. And, whereas the Ripper has been celebrated far and wide in the songs of the rock 'n' roll era, the Axman made his musical mark at the very height of his criminal spree, with a song that he all but caused to have been written.

So why has nobody ever recorded it?

"I dunno." I heard that answer so many times that I eventually gave up asking people.

The facts of the case of the Mysterious Axman are simple. On the morning of May 22, 1918, police were called to a home in one of the city's poorer quarters, to be confronted by the bodies of a local baker, Joseph Maggio, and his wife, Catherine, lying brutally hacked on their blood-soaked double bed.

There was no question as to how the killer entered the house — a panel had been carefully chiseled out of the back door. Nor was there any doubt as to the cause of death; a bloody ax stood in the bathtub. A few doors down the road, a chalk-written message declared, mystifyingly, "Mrs. Joseph Maggio will sit up tonight. Just write Mrs. Toney."

Beyond those, however, no clues remained — and neither would they in any of the similar slayings that lay ahead. A month after the Maggios were slain, grocer Louis Bossumer and his common-law wife, Annie Harriet Lowe, were attacked but, miraculously, not killed; in August, a woman named Mrs. Edward Schneider awoke just as the Axman swung his weapon – she, too, survived the assault. But a few nights later, the killer returned to his murderous ways with the slaying of a grocer, Joseph Romano.

Hysteria swept the city. The only leads the police had to go on were all the victims were Italian, all worked either as a grocer or a baker, and all the murders appeared to have been committed by a character whom the *New Orleans Times-Picayune* described as "the greatest bogeyman that New Orleans has ever known."

A bogeyman is precisely what he was. With no clue as to who, or even what, he was, the Axman took on every conceivable shade of identity.

He was the London Ripper, emerging from his bloodstained retirement to revel again in the gore of the innocent!

He was a madman, escaped from one of the state's lunatic asylums, or maybe he'd never even been placed into one.

He was God's punishment on a sinful city — although even the religious were hard-pressed to explain why the Lord would be conducting a vendetta against the grocery community.

He was any of so many past victims of New Orleans' lawlessness, or maybe one of its perpetrators — a pirate, a rapist, a murderer, a thug.

Or maybe he was none of these things and all of them, some unknown supernatural entity, conjured up from the depths of hell, or raised from the deepest recesses of the bayou, not even a man at all. Or not a complete man. Then as now, the bayou reverberated to the legends of the half-human, half-*something* horrors in its midst, and the only thing that stopped these beings from entering the city in search of prey was — what? As the panic reached its peak, a terrified populace could think of no good reason at all why the secrets of the swamp should not become the scourge of the city, and the longer the Axman eluded the police, the more it seemed likely that he always would. How do you even handcuff a ghoul?

Across town, families divided their nights into segments and took turns to stand guard while the other members slept. Shotgun sales soared, and armed citizens walked the streets day and night, eyes peeled for anyone who fit the admittedly vague descriptions offered by the survivors of the Mysterious Axman's wrath or who appeared to be acting in a suspicious nature. Many was the innocent who found himself confronted by armed vigilantes and forced, at gunpoint, to state his business; many, too, one imagines, were the regular housebreakers, adulterers and other secret travelers who were forced to give up their sinful ways, at least for the time being.

The improved vigilance appears to have saved at least one life; on August 11, one Al Durand stepped outside his back door one morning to find an ax and chisel neatly arranged on the ground and sure signs that an attempt had been made to break in. Later in the month, grocer Joseph LeBouef himself scared the attacker away after he was awakened by the sound of his door being assaulted; the following morning, yet another grocer, Paul Lobella, returned home after a night away to find his door had been chiseled through.

Another grocer, Paul Durel, was spared because he had the foresight, or luck, to leave a case of tomatoes against the very panel that the Mysterious Axman tried to cut through.

That was on September 15, and, as the year rolled on, it appeared as though the Mysterious Axman had vanished as suddenly and, indeed, mysteriously as he had arrived. Into the new year he remained a memory. Life returned to normal, sleep patterns went back to how they used to be. And then the Mysterious Axman reappeared in Gretna, and the city trembled again. Except now the terror was about to take on a new dimension. Not only was he, as the local newspaper spat, "a bloodthirsty maniac, filled with a passion for human slaughter," he also loved jazz.

Or so he said in a letter to that same journal, datemarked Hell on March 13, 1919, in which he also offered the terrified city a most peculiar bargain.

> *Esteemed Mortal:*
>
> *They have never caught me and they never will. They have never seen me, for I am invisible, even as the ether that surrounds your earth. I am not a human being, but a spirit and a demon from the hottest hell. I am what you Orleanians and your foolish police call the Axman.*
>
> *When I see fit, I shall come and claim other victims. I alone know whom they shall be. I shall leave no clue except my bloody ax, besmeared with blood and brains of he whom I have sent below to keep me company.*
>
> *If you wish you may tell the police to be careful not to rile me. Of course, I am a reasonable spirit. I take no offense at the way they have conducted their investigations in the past. In fact, they have been so utterly stupid as to not only amuse me, but His Satanic Majesty, Francis Josef, etc. But tell them to beware. Let them not try to discover what I am, for it were better that they were never born than to incur*

the wrath of the Axman. I don't think there is any need of such a warning, for I feel sure the police will always dodge me, as they have in the past. They are wise and know how to keep away from all harm.

Undoubtedly, you Orleanians think of me as a most horrible murderer, which I am, but I could be much worse if I wanted to. If I wished, I could pay a visit to your city every night. At will I could slay thousands of your best citizens, for I am in close relationship with the Angel of Death.

Now, to be exact, at 12:15 (earthly time) on next Tuesday night, I am going to pass over New Orleans. In my infinite mercy, I am going to make a little proposition to you people. Here it is: I am very fond of jazz music, and I swear by all the devils in the nether regions that every person shall be spared in whose home a jazz band is in full swing at the time I have just mentioned. If everyone has a jazz band going, well, then, so much the better for you people. One thing is certain and that is that some of your people who do not jazz it on Tuesday night (if there be any) will get the ax.

Well, as I am cold and crave the warmth of my native Tartarus, and it is about time I leave your earthly home, I will cease my discourse. Hoping that thou wilt publish this, that it may go well with thee, I have been, am and will be the worst spirit that ever existed either in fact or realm of fancy.

He signed his missive "the Axman."

The following Tuesday, the entire city poured out to accede to the Axman's wishes. Restaurants, clubs and niteries the entire city over were packed with dancers and musicians. Private parties were arranged, and opened to all comers, each of them determined to "jazz it up." There was not a musician in New Orleans or beyond who did not have at least one booking for the night, and many had several, racing from house to house to club to bar, their instrument

Sheet music for what has to be one of the most opportunistic songs ever written. One wonders what the Axman himself thought about it?

in hand, to help protect the city from the Axman's curse.

That was when a song was composed to honor the Axman and mark the occasion, an instrumental piece hurriedly printed by the local World's Music Publishing of 413 Godchaux Building, New Orleans. "The Mysterious Axman's Jazz" was written by the publishing company's own president, Joseph J. Davilla, the author of other local favorites "If You Were My Spider and I Were Your Fly" and the riotous "Give Me Back My Husband, You've Had Him Long Enuff." Sheet music for this latest composition sold as quickly as WMP could print it. More than any other single piece of music performed that night, "The Mysterious Axman's Jazz" rang out over the entire city.

The Axman was true to his word; he did not return that night. But no matter how fervently New Orleanians might have prayed and continued to play for deliverance, he remained murderously at large. Perhaps he was not, as sundry investigators have since suggested, responsible for a late-night ax attack on a young girl named Sarah Laumann on August 3, 1919; she was not Italian, she had nothing to do with grocers or bakers, and her attacker used a window, not a door panel, to gain entry. But the attack reawakened all the old fears, and, if the Axman had been taking a break, the knowledge that there was now a copycat killer on the prowl seems to have awakened him to further mischief.

A week later, the Mysterious Axman used all his traditional tricks to break into a home on Elysian Fields Avenue and attack a man named Steve Boca; he survived, and so did a druggist, William Carson, who was able to fire off a couple of shots at a man who had just entered his home, ax in hand, through a door panel. And, in October, grocer Mike Pepitone was savagely butchered while he slept and with such stealth that his wife and six children, asleep in the next room, were not even aware of the killing until morning.

That was the end of the Mysterious Axman's reign, but why — nobody knows. Perhaps he died, perhaps he simply tired of the slaughter. Or perhaps he moved away . . . two years later, in 1921, Mike Pepitone's widow, Esther Albano, was arrested in San Bernadino, California, for the murder of a small-time Crescent City blackmailer, a pharmacist named "Doc" Joseph Mumfre, whom she insisted not only was the Axman, but who had also murdered her second husband, Angelo Albano.

There was no shortage of circumstantial evidence. Unrelated, it was said, to the 1918 killings, there had been a flurry of otherwise similar ax murders in New Orleans in 1911. The police at that time insisted they were Mafia related, but did admit that they stopped only when Mumfre himself was sent to jail on a completely unrelated matter, to serve a sentence that ended, with parole, in May 1918, shortly before the first in the next round of murders. Mumfre then left New Orleans for a new life on the West Coast the following September, immediately following Pepitone's death.

The police were never, officially, able to make the connection between Mumfre and the murders, and sundry freelance investigators have done sterling work debunking, for example, the 1911 ax attacks. But still Mumfre (or Mumphrey, Monfre or even Manfre, as he has also been termed) remains the closest thing any of them have to a suspect, which simply isn't enough to prevent the Mysterious Axman from becoming Louisiana's own Jack the Ripper. Or remaining something even more dangerous, evil and primeval.

Because what is to say that those people were mistaken, those superstitious millions who cowered in their homes that season, or who jazzed it up for one long night in the belief . . . or maybe just the desperate hope . . . that music could save their lives?

Something *was* at large in the streets of their city, hacking and chopping the people to death, and something was at large in the bayou as well, because almost everyone knew somebody who had vanished in its depths.

And it might even still be in there.

TRACK EIGHTEEN

"Bad Things" by Jace Everett
from the LP *Jace Everett* (Sony)
2005

A HUGE FISH. Mr. Martial Ogeron gives us the following description of a monster of the finny tribe lately killed by him off the mouth of the Lafourche in the breakers: Length of the body from point of nose to the tail, 14 ft; length of tail, 6 ft; extreme width on the back, 20 ft; thickness from top of back to bottom of belly, 7 feet; width of mouth 3 feet 6 inches, with horns on either side, 3 feet long; cavity of brain, 9 by 16 inches.

This huge monster, when killed, was lying with his month open catching small fish, on which it is supposed to subsist. It was shot through the head at the distance of about five paces, and immediately sunk to the bottom. It was then fastened to, and towed in to shore, where it was dissected for the purpose of being converted to oil; but a storm arising, the captor was forced to abandon the project and fly for safety. Its liver, was the size of a rice cask. The exterior of this fish was covered with a skin resembling more that of an elephant than anything else to which we can compare it.

> *Mr. Ogeron is a seafaring man, and says he has
> never before seen a fish of this description in our waters.
> What kind of a fish is it, and where did it come from? Let
> us hear from you, naturalists!*
>
> From the *Thibodaux Minerva*, 1856

Modern opinion (and, indeed, some contemporary observers) insist Mr. Ogeron's catch was either a devil ray or a manatee, either of which could have been swept into the river by any of the area's recent storms — in particular, the so-called Last Island storm of August 9–10, 1856, which was described that same weekend as the most powerful storm in living memory. As it turns out, that was a little like christening the *Titanic* as the most unsinkable ship there had ever been, for just a couple of weeks later, along came the Southeastern States Hurricane, and it blew every last memory of the Last Island storm away. But not every memory of the monster. There are some things that science can't explain away, even after the scientists have all said their piece. Swamp monsters, for example.

Personally, I've always been more partial to the less alarmist but equally resonant term coined by the late John A. Keel, author of *Strange Creatures from Time and Space*. "Abominable Swamp Slobs," he called them, before continuing, "There's hardly a respectable swamp in the Deep South that does not boast at least one ASS." There is definitely a less-than-respectful pun in that sentence, of course, although this is probably not the time to mention the ASS's closest acronymical relative, the Really Exciting Diluvian Necronym Existing in Cypress Kaos.

Keel then outlines several of his favorite ASS-sites and sightings, and it may or may not have been coincidental that, less than a year after *Strange Creatures from Time and Space* was published, DC Comics commenced the run of its own bog beast, *Swamp Thing*.

Swamp Thing is the archetypal modern bayou legend. Originally created by Len Wein (co-parent, too, to Marvel's Wolverine) and Bernie Wrightson (designer of the second-best-ever Meat Loaf album cover, *Dead Ringer*), Swamp Thing was once a scientist, Doctor Alec Holland. Working to perfect a "bio-restorative" formula that could have reversed most of the causes of modern global warming, Holland was about to perfect his work when a bomb destroyed his laboratory and covered his body in acid and flames. He threw himself into the mud and undergrowth, and the formula began to work. By the time he arose, he *was* the mud and undergrowth.

Swamp Thing debuted in the *House of Secrets* horror mag in July 1971, flourished via Wein's own comic book from 1972 to 1976, and has been making intermittent comebacks ever since, with each new author allowing the legend to spread a little further afield and a forgettable movie, Wes Craven's *Swamp Thing* (1982), to make sure that we didn't forget him.

By the mid-1980s, the character was even in the hands of Alan Moore, one of modern comicdom's most gifted visionaries, and legend be damned. Moore interwove an entire mythology, placing the Swamp Thing that today's readers know and love (and maybe slightly recoil from) as just the latest in a long line of the things, hundreds of Swamp Things over the centuries who are the designated defenders of an elemental community called "the Green," through which all the planet's plant life is connected.

Frankly, it didn't strike *me* as one of Moore's best ideas, either, particularly since it played havoc with the otherwise more or less seamless continuity that had been maintained by old Swampie's other masterminds; a less-than-half-man, half-vegetable creation born when scientist Alex Olsen was caught in an explosion in his laboratory, who now battled evil, industry and all-purpose baddies in order to protect the pristine boundaries of his bayou home.

That said, Moore's approach is generally regarded to have completely overhauled the world of American comics, paving the way

A graphic novel recounts the first adventures of Alan Moore's Swamp Thing.

for the adult-themed titles that would soon provide the industry with some of its best-loved writers and themes, and finally dismissing any lingering notion that they'd even been written for kids in the first place. (It may also have inspired Manchester indie band the Chameleons' equally inspired "Swamp Thing.")

In the years since then, Swamp Thing has avenged his wife's murder, had a daughter, hung out with Jesus, battled the Antichrist, been killed, suffered from a split personality, fought alongside Batman . . . and the last we heard, been canceled due to low sales. Well, if they can do it to She-Hulk, they can do it to Swamp Thing.

The real bayou, of course . . . the one that might look like that which a stream of artists have built around Swamp Thing, but which has no time whatsoever for any concept whatsoever of good and evil . . . the real bayou secretes beings of its own which apparently make Swampie look like Aunt Petunia's award-winning pot plant. And they've been around a lot longer, as well.

I was six years old in suburban England the first time I truly became aware of what lives around here — watching an episode of *Thunderbirds*, Gerry Anderson's Supermarionation series about the adventures of International Rescue, called to the heart of an isolated swamp to do battle with giant alligators.

Like Swampie, they weren't a natural phenomenon. No, they were created by an avaricious boatman named Culp, after he hears his scientist employer discussing a marvelous new potion he's just discovered that could affect the growth rate of any living thing. The scientist thinks it could help end world hunger; Culp realizes it could make him rich. So he steals a vial, but spills some into the sink. He washes it away, it goes straight into the river, and, hey presto, three enormous reptiles are attacking the house.

International Rescue ultimately save the day, of course. But even they would be powerless if they were called upon to defend the world against everything that can bite and scratch and snap and nibble in the waters around here.

Mermaids have long been said to be resident as far afield as the Bayou Manchac and in and around Maurepas and Head of Island, Louisiana, although they are sadly less attested to than those that dwell on the Pascagoula River in Mississippi next door — home, also, to a trio of five-foot-tall lobstermen who descended from a flying saucer in October 1973 and half-scared a couple of catfish-fishermen to death. But that's another story for another journey, because Louisiana has its own share of night-crawling nasties, beginning with the Loup Carou (or loup-garou, or rougarou . . . it has almost as many names as there are differing descriptions of it), which has apparently been around since the beginning of human memory and maybe of humanity itself.

Once, it is said, it was a human child, lost or abandoned in the depths of the bayou. Though Loup Carou is a Cajun term (one that more recent lore has muddled up with the werewolf), the Native Americans who lived here knew it as the Letiche: a human child indeed, but one which was taken in by alligators, which raised the babe as their own, taught it their own behavior and mannerisms, until it had grown into a vast flesh-eating half-man, half-reptilian monstrosity.

METAIRIE CEMETERY, SHOWING FINE TOMBS, NEW ORLEANS, LA.

Another more modern variant on the story tells of a train wreck in the early years of the 20th century, involving one of the traveling carnivals that then toured the area. Catapulted from the wreckage as it crashed from the tracks, many of the escaped animals either died from their injuries or fell prey to the swamp. But a troupe of chimpanzees was hardier. They survived, they flourished — and they bred with the alligators to create, again, a vast flesh-eating half-man-like, half-reptilian monstrosity.

Such creatures and tales, as John A. Keel pointed out, abound throughout the region. But nowhere is this legend more pronounced and more attested to than in the depths of a primordial backwater morass known as the Honey Island Swamp.

Less than an hour outside of New Orleans, the Honey Island Swamp has been described as being virtually untainted by modern man, and when one considers how many hunters, hikers and extreme paranormal investigators the area now attracts, that is quite an achievement. Even the tour boats that escort the tourists through the overhanging cypress and the still, muddy waters tend to blend in with the wilderness, and the guides will happily reel off the wildlife that calls the swamp its undisturbed home — alligators, raccoons, owls, wild boars, coypu, snakes, turtles, bald eagles, black bears and even an ivory-billed woodpecker, a bird that was officially considered extinct until 2004 (before being rediscovered in the nearby Pearl River Wildlife Management Area).

There is, of course, a good reason for the swamp's survival. Over 20 miles long and nearly seven miles across, there are parts that are so impenetrable they are impossible to reach; other areas are accessible by boat, or maybe on foot. The swamp is also close to NASA's top-secret Stennis Space Center, which further restricts casual access. But the heart of the swamp contains secrets that neither scientists nor naturalists have truly cracked, and maybe they never will.

In 1974, however, a pair of off-duty air traffic controllers, Harlan E. Ford and Ray Mills, came close to one of them. The two men were hunting in the swamp when they came across the body of a wild boar, its throat torn open by something immensely powerful — and heavy enough to have left its vast, apelike footprints embedded deep in the soft soil around the corpse. The hunters were still examining the prints when something made them look up across the clearing. There they saw, standing upright on two legs, a humanoid creature coated in gray, dingy hair, over seven feet tall and weighing in the region of 500 pounds. Its deep and wide-set eyes were an unblinking yellow — and it stunk.

"It was like nothing I'd ever seen before," Ford said of the encounter. "Ugly and sinister and looking like something out of a horror movie. It swung around and looked at us for a moment, then tore off into the swamp. I want you to know it scared the heck out of me!"

Theirs was not the first such encounter, either here or elsewhere in the bayou. Indeed, 11 years earlier, the same two men emerged from the same swamp convinced they had seen something completely unknown and possibly unnatural lurking in the undergrowth. Their report was dismissed at the time — they probably just caught a glimpse of a bear. This time, however, they were believed, and their sighting would not be the last.

But the visitor to Louisiana swiftly discovers that you don't need to be trekking through a tractless marsh many miles from civilization in order to confront the inexplicable. Britney Spears grew up in Louisiana, after all, and her success strikes some people as being just as baffling as the mere existence of the Abominable Swamp Slob. Almost every town, village or long-drowned cluster of shacks in the region can boast of its own nocturnal terror, swirling through what was once the main street of a tiny community. Drifting through the foundations of what used to be someone's house. Or taking a short cut through a cemetery because it was there first.

Places like these would be a great location for a horror movie. Except, of course, it's already been done — every time another Hollywood moneybags figures there's gold in dem dere dead bodies and whistles up a New Orleans crew to prepare for another nocturnal shoot. Screened in the United States in November 2009, the A&E cable network even dispatched its *Extreme Paranormal* investigative team down to a graveyard in Manchac Swamp to commune with the victims of Frenier's Aunt Julia and treat viewers to a prime-time half hour of jumbled voodoo, mini-cam entombment and the kind of outrageous exaggerations that only reality TV can supply. I didn't take notes as I watched the show, but I'm pretty sure that the presenters claimed that single burial ground was stuffed with more corpses than the storm caused across the whole of the state.

In fact, Manchac is scarcely representative of any Louisiana graveyard, if only because its residents are firmly entombed underground. Elsewhere, for first-time viewers, and even the seasoned cemetery gazer, there's something indescribably unearthly about the average bayou necropolis.

Maybe it's the fact that it looms rather than lurks. Maybe it's the knowledge that the dead you've come to walk past lie not at your feet, poised to reach up through the soil to grab at your ankles, but

Vaults of Old St. Louis Cemetery
New Orleans, La.

Floral offerings at the Old St Louis cemetery.

at your elbow or shoulder, just a sudden skeletal lunge away from your throat. They may not be Living, they may not be Grateful, and they certainly are not Evil. But still the Dead here have a bead on life that no other boneyard in the country could match. Or envy.

There's more, too. No matter that you know what to expect, because the tour brochures took all the shock from the sight, still the knowledge that you are now standing so far below sea level that the water lies just inches beneath your feet is a sobering one. Why else would the dead be buried above ground, and why else would Louisiana have such a rich storehouse of vampire legends?

The day we returned to New Orleans, there seemed to be a Gothic convention in town; either that, or we'd wandered into the center of a Jace Everett fan club convention. Or the same download playing *ad nauseam*.

Indiana-born country singer Jace Everett recorded "Bad Things" in 2005, when he cut his first album, *Jace Everett*. And there, he admitted, it might have remained were it not for "a really cool story of synchronicity." He explained, "my friends at iTunes gave me the

OLD ST. LOUIS CEMETERY, NEW ORLEANS, LA. — 15

A less well-kept view of the Old St Louis cemetery.

opportunity to be the iTunes Single of the Week in 2006. So 'Bad Things' was downloaded by about 210,000 people, and one of those people happened to be Alan Ball, the creator of *True Blood*."

Ball originally intended the song as a simple placeholder to accompany the show's credits during the production phase, until musical supervisor Gary Calamar found something more suitable. Except he couldn't. "Jace's song has a great mix of menace, humor, wit and wild romance," Calamar raved. "Against the opening sequence, it was wickedly badass."

Everett was riffing around a Steve Earle tune, "Poor Boy," when he came up with "Bad Things," but he twisted it out of its original major key "and gave it a darker vibe, which led me to the lyric and melody." There were certainly no vampires on his mind at the time. "The initial idea was one of violence and vengeance. A guy owed me money, and I wanted to do 'bad things to you' in the original lyric.

"About 10 minutes into it, I realized it was coming off more sexy than scary and that '[I wanna do bad things] to you' sounded a little creepy; date rape . . . not good! So I changed the lyric to 'with you.'

Oddly enough, half the people who hear the song [still] think I sing 'to you.' But I don't.'"

Maybe they just wish he would, and if you sing the wrong words loud enough, even Tinkerbell might rise from the grave. But even with the correct lyric, it remains a sexy, creepy song, and it doesn't really matter that Bon Temps itself is far outside of the bayou loop (or it would be, if it existed). The show's opening credits, a patchwork of images that sews up every cliché that the swamp has ever suffered, make for the kind of music video that most artists would trade their grannies in for. And that's both grannies, not just the one that smells of cabbage.

So yeah, "Bad Things" is what you hear as you drive up to the cemetery, and the pictures that play in your mind in the dark — the rotting shack, the waiting 'gator, the posing Klansmen, the decaying possum — they're all in there as well. But there's something else waiting, something that you can't quite put your finger on because, although you know what you think you're hoping to find, be it the Vampire Lestat or Sheriff Eric's statuesque friend Pam, you know that you're also hoping that you won't.

It was Anne Rice who popularized the concept of ageless nosferatus running loose round Louisiana when she inserted the Vampire Lestat and his cronies into the heart of New Orleans in 1976. But it was no fluke of geographical convenience that prompted her to set her tale there rather than any of the other American cities with which popular fiction has gifted its bloodsuckers: Castle Rock, Maine (Stephen King's *Salem's Lot*); New York City (Whitley Strieber's *The Hunger*); Forks, Washington (Stephenie Meyer's *Twilight*); and so on. Long before *Interview with the Vampire* ignited the cottage industry that Anne Rice's "Vampire Chronicles" would become, the city and its surroundings not only knew the vampire's kiss, they welcomed it. Because it made the locals feel at home.

New Orleans itself was largely settled by immigrants escaping a Europe that, in the 1700s, was beset by vampire legend. It took only a mildly morbid mind to consider that not all of the new arrivals were leaving their traditions and beliefs behind. Especially when one visited the docks and saw the long, casket-like boxes which the French, in particular, seemed to favor for their luggage. Nor the apparent stealth and secrecy with which the city's rich and powerful secluded their newly built homes, behind great screens of foliage and towering walls. Under such circumstances, it simply stood to reason that one of those dark, foreboding mansions should be thus remarked for good reason.

For example, early in the 1830s, a new family moved into a house on Bourbon Street. Alberto De Leonne was an immigrant who arrived from Santo Domingo with his wife, a breathtaking quadroon named Clothilde, and her brother Ramon, whose duties included tending the beautiful gardens that De Leonne had arranged.

Ramon loved the garden, but that was his only sober interest in life. A drinker whose favorite tipple was absinthe and a laudanum addict as well, Ramon was a familiar sight around the bars and alleyways of the Old Quarter. It was in one of these alleys that he is said to have disturbed a secret voodoo ritual. A curse was flung upon him, and Ramon, as susceptible to fear as he was to all his other vices, withdrew completely from society.

Always a late riser, he now took to sleeping the entire day away, rising only as the sun went down and then returning to bed as it rose again. All night long, though, he could be heard working in the garden, and, when his lifeless body was discovered one day, tangled in the roots of a Spanish lime tree, it seemed only honorable to bury him in the grounds he had adored despite everything. It was only as his grave was being prepared that the servants discovered precisely how Ramon had been filling those long nights that he spent in the garden, as decomposed body after body came to light. The entire property, it seemed, had been transformed into one vast charnel house, but it was the police who revealed the most chilling aspect of the affair. Every single body had been drained of blood before being buried.

You can see why so many fictional vampires seem to call New Orleans home!

With the garden now considered a crime scene, Ramon was eventually laid to rest in De Leonne's family plot. But the servants swore that he still walked the grounds and refused even to consider any duties that might take them close to the garden after dark. Finally, an exasperated De Leonne vowed to put an end to such foolishness. He settled down to keep an overnight vigil and was killed as brutally and miserably as any of the poor souls whose corpses had been found interred in the garden.

But Ramon did not escape. Awakened by the sounds of a disturbance, De Leonne's eldest son and a servant, Sadugh, rushed to the conservatory, where they were able to capture and bind the walking dead man. Other servants hurried to the scene to dig a makeshift grave around the writhing, prone Ramon; then, when Sadugh deemed the pit was deep enough, he took a vast iron nail and thrust it through the creature's heart, pinning it to the ground. The stake was hammered home, and New Orleans' first vampire was finally dead.

Ramon would not be the last — so-called vampire murders have haunted New Orleans for over 200 years; there were even a couple of arrests in the early 1900s, two brothers who were tried, found guilty and sentenced to death. But the murders continued following the executions, and when a judge ordered their crypt opened, both of the bodies had vanished. Nor would Ramon be the most famous. For all the indignities that actors Tom Cruise and Brad Pitt would perpetrate upon Anne Rice's original vision, *Interview with the Vampire* told a tale that has now been absorbed into the New Orleans DNA, and Sookie Stackhouse carried the bloodsucker even deeper into the regional psyche, to the fictional town of Bon Temps, which itself could be almost any small town in rural northern Louisiana. Except for the high incidence of other supernatural beings that seem to be attracted to it.

Again, however, the fiction has its roots in truth. You can still stumble upon (or, at least, have pointed out to you) older homesteads whose keyholes have been inserted upside down, as a protection against the undead. And, though vampire Bill Compton may not have existed, both his manners and his backstory — fighting in the Civil War when he was "turned" by a woman from whom he sought shelter — could have slipped out of any of many local legends. Ghosts from that conflict abound, after all. Why shouldn't there be vampires, werewolves, loup carous, flesh eaters and monster fish as well?

Why can't there be ghosts and 'gators, figures of legend and legends of figures, lepers and lunatics, zombies and zombi? Amos Moses and Marie Laveau, Dr. John and Doctor John, carnies and critters, hookers and howlers, Mysterious Axemen and mud-soaked corpses and a veritable pantechnicon of other crazy things, including some we forgot to look out for, or didn't know were here, or were just too damned caught up in one thing to even think of going looking somewhere else for another.

And whether or not we ever found what we were looking for, or if we even knew what it was to begin with, the last day of our Louisiana vacation ends in much the same way as the first day began, with Highway 61 stretching eternally in front of us, and the car stereo booming out the songs that we programmed in a lifetime ago.

"Maybe when we get home," Amy asks me, "you could find something else to listen to?"

EPILOGUE

You don't really believe that's the end of the story, do you?

That we came all this way and didn't spend at least a few nights on Bourbon Street or a few more dancing Mardi Gras away? That we didn't sit in a bar in a backwater someplace, listening to real, authentic Cajun music being played by (and for) people who understood every word they sang, and that we didn't go to New Orleans Zoo to retrace the footsteps of Nastassja Kinski, so radiant through the remake of the B movie horror *Cat People*? Jesus, I can hear you thinking, you went all that way and you didn't once think of *that*?

How about *No Mercy*, then? The first time I ever went to New Orleans, I tell Amy, I watched them filming a scene for that, standing on a corner while machines showered rain down onto the street. Didn't see Kim Basinger, though, or even Richard Gere.

It doesn't really matter, though. This is not a book about movies, because they already tell you what you think you are seeing. Music makes you work harder for that thrill, asks you to turn off all your other senses and let your imagination take you there instead.

That's one of the threads that runs through this travelogue — imagination and the ease with which it can transport us to a different place, whether or not we've even been there before. I close my eyes, and I see all these places, but you only have my word for it that I was actually there. You could make the same journey without leaving your armchair, and hopefully — if you've actually read this far — you did.

Because that's why this can't be the end of the tale. I mean, I don't want to get all Neil Sedaka's 1970s comeback on you, but all I've done is told you that's where the music takes me. It could easily take you someplace else entirely, or it might not take you anywhere at all, because — as I somewhat self-defeatingly noted at the beginning of our journey — the only thing that really unites the songs that play at the head of each chapter is the fact that I happened to have them all handy.

But that's only part of the reason why. Because it's also true that a lot of what we visited here, or went searching for, has simply vanished off the face of the earth. The physical landmarks may still be there, or the scars that were left when they vanished — capricious weather and cold, hard progress aren't the only wrecking balls around, after all. But the people who remember the older stories or who have the local know-how to invent a few new ones are also disappearing to be replaced by a generation that (or so we are told by their elders) cares nothing for the relics of a life they never knew, because they're too busy forging one from the things that they do understand.

In less than the space of a quarter of a century, an entire way of life has been supplanted with another, not just in Louisiana, but all across America — across the globe, in fact. Twenty years ago, our streets weren't surmounted by cell-phone towers, our days weren't consumed by computers and the Internet, and, though our nights were already wall-to-wall television, it wasn't broadcast to wall-to-wall television screens.

But two decades' worth of children grew up knowing nothing else, and when progress leads us someplace so fast, the past cannot help but fall behind.

There will always be people who continue to care for the preservation of the past, their heritage and their cultural background. There's a nostalgia industry to make sure of that, and it doesn't matter what kind of old memory you're hoping to recapture. If you can't find the real McCoy, pop down to the mall. Someone's bound to have manufactured a genuine reproduction, and you might even get a certificate of authenticity with it.

The stories that the bayou tells are the original items, even the ones that were only just created. I don't believe for a moment that Blind Joe Reynolds met Marie Laveau, alive or dead or in any state between. I'm not convinced that there's a ghostly paddle steamer still chugging up and down a long-forgotten cut-off; and, while I concede that there may be an Abominable Swamp Slob in the Honey Island Swamp, the only true ASSES around here are those of us who go unseeingly about our daily business, not noticing until it's too damned late that the cute little diner that used to stand on the corner has been swallowed up by a new multiplex, which itself will be brick dust in a couple of years, when the developers sell up because nobody goes there, and someone else opens a mega-church in its place.

Cities change, landscapes change, they always have, and they always will. Nobody, not even the most blinkered conservationist, would really want to replan our cities as they were 50 years ago, or strip back our amenities to the days of candles and horsepower. The modern world has given us too much that is invaluable, that does make things easier, and which has made a difference to our quality of life.

But it's also given us a lot of background noise, the static of so many other innovations, screaming out of our TV commercials, or bellowing out of the stores down the road, a constant and ceaseless cacophony designed with just one purpose in mind. To convince us that it doesn't matter how well something we already possess might work, somebody's found a new way of doing the same thing for three times the price. Plus, it comes in a very nice box.

We will all be in very nice boxes one day — and, if we're lucky, there won't be a hurricane blowing through town to strip them away before we're decently buried. What would make us even luckier, though, would be if every single one of us was to pause at some point before then and just make a note of the things that matter.

The stupid tales that Grandma tells of how things were when she was a child. The way a certain candy tasted, or the color of the leaves on the trees in the park before the pollution turned them all to stumps and another well-meaning citizens' action group carved them to sawdust just in case a child got a splinter while he climbed on them.

Remember the slang that you used as a child, the comics you loved and the stories you read. Take photographs of everything that isn't nailed into place, and then take more of the things that are. And write, write, write about everything you see, because it's only through words that anything survives, and it's only through its survival that we'll remember how much it once mattered.

That's what this book was really all about: carving out a tiny niche of memory that might mean nothing to anybody else, or which may mean the world to everyone, and holding it aloft because it really is important. And hoping that, if everyone who reads it did the same thing themselves, then we might be able to hold on to the things that the rest of the planet is sweeping away.

Half of the music that is discussed in this book I still own on vinyl. A couple of songs were on 8-track, and one was on a reel-to-reel. Right there lies a world that has vanished, no matter how gallantly the LP record may be trying to stage a comeback. And on the other side of the technological coin, two of the books I referred to in my research were most readily available on Google Books, so there's a world that's supplanting another.

It's the little things. So long as you keep up your cell-phone coverage and don't go with one of those companies whose range decreases the farther you get from their showroom, it's really difficult to get lost in the bayou today. You just call for help or check your GPS, and that's great, but it's also disappointing as well. Getting lost is half the fun of going places because it's often when you're lost that you find the best things.

Like the funny little bookshop in that town you don't remember, where you bought that old, old guidebook that you since found for $10 less on the Internet. But if you hadn't gone there, you wouldn't remember the smell of the books, or the warmth of the dust as it danced on the sunlight on that pile of old *Harper's,* and you certainly wouldn't have browsed through them and discovered the writings of Lafcadio Hearn, in whose footsteps this book would dearly love to tread.

Like the houseboat rotting at its mooring in a creek with river mud creeping up to the deck, but still enough living space for someone to call it home, because they'd rather live there than anyplace else.

Like the old man selling bric-a-brac from a trestle table on the roadside, who didn't have a clue how you should get to where you were going, but who was happy to sell you an 1861 silver half dollar, minted in New Orleans on the eve of Louisiana's secession from the union, maybe shortly after, or even under the auspices of the Confederacy. It's the only American coin to be struck under three separate governments, and, although there's no way of knowing which one is which, the romantic in all of us will have its own idea.

Like the reasons why that romance even matters anymore.

There's 20 years' worth of getting lost bound up in these pages, 20 years of hearing odd tales and chasing old legends, and 20 years of following the indescribable feeling that I get when I listen to a certain pile of disconnected old songs.

I'm still not convinced that I caught up with it, though, and I'm not sure that I really want to. The very best dreams are often the ones that you simply cannot lay your finger on, and if there was a blinding revelation at the end of this journey, a stone tablet or even a glittering grail of some description, we must have driven straight past it.

And that was probably the best thing we could have done.

The bayous we can visit are already being destroyed. The bayou we imagine is safest underground.

ACKNOWLEDGMENTS

From barmen to bellhops, concierge to cleaner, traffic cop to construction worker, there are a lot of people who helped get this book off the ground because they helped us get around. Thanks to everyone I met and passed a moment with, whether or not they remember it, because without at least one of you, we'd probably still be parked by that crossroads outside Thibodaux, wondering which of the two northbound lanes is the left-hand fork.

And then . . . to Jen Hale, Emily Schultz, and all at ECW — we meet again.

To Amy Hanson. Well, I never said I knew how to drive.

Et aussi, Jo-Ann Greene, Jen W., Linda and Larry, Deb and Roger, Dave and Sue, Oliver, Toby and Trevor, Karen and Todd, and Jenny D.R. Hi to the Lowes and hello to the Hyatts. Anchorite Man, Bateerz and family, Chrissie Bentley, Blind Pew, Mrs. B. East, J.D., Mrs. Nose and family, Gef the Talking Mongoose, the Gremlins who live in the heat pump, Geoff Monmouth, Naughty Miranda, Nutkin, the Shecklers who showed up as the last chapter was completed, a lot of Thompsons, and Neville Viking.

BIBLIOGRAPHY

Alongside and in addition to the titles and publications referenced in the text, the following provided hours of happy reading and research during the time it took to write this book.

Fiction

Everett, Peter: *Bellocq's Women* (Random House, 2001)

McCloud, Lady Alice: *Whalebone Strict* (Nexus, 2007)

Moore, Alan, et al.: *Saga of the Swamp Thing* (Vertigo, 1987)

Rhodes, Jewell P: *Voodoo Dreams: A Novel of Marie Laveau* (Picador, 1995)

Rice, Anne: *Interview with the Vampire* (Alfred A. Knopf, 1976)

Roberts, Nora: *Midnight Bayou* (Putnam, 2001)

Nonfiction

Ancelet, Barry Jean: *Cajun and Creole Folktales* (University Press of Mississippi, 1994)

Baum, Dan: *Nine Lives — Death & Life in New Orleans* (Spiegel & Grau, 2009)

Bordowitz, Hank: *Bad Moon Rising: The Unauthorized History of Creedence Clearwater Revival* (Chicago Review Press, 2007)

Brown, Cecil: *Stagolee Shot Billy* (Harvard University Press, 2003)

Cott, Jonathan: *Wandering Ghost: The Odyssey of Lafcadio Hearn* (Knopf, 1991)

De Caro, Frank (editor): *Louisiana Sojourns — Travelers' Tales & Literary Journeys* (Louisiana State University, 1998)

Dr. John, with Rummel, Jack: *Under a Hoodoo Moon* (St. Martin's Press, 1994)

Egan, Sean: *Animal Tracks — The Story of the Animals, Newcastle's Rising Suns* (Helter Skelter, 2001)

Ferris, William: *Blues from the Delta* (Da Capo Press, 1998)

Hanson, Amy: *Kicking against the Pricks: An Armchair Guide to Nick Cave* (Helter Skelter, 2005)

Hedin, Benjamin (editor): *Studio A — The Bob Dylan Reader* (W. W. Norton, 2004)

Horwitz, Tony: *A Voyage Long and Strange* (Henry Holt, 2008)

Keel, John A.: *Strange Creatures from Time and Space* (Fawcett Gold Medal, 1970)

Lester, Julius: *Black Folktales* (Grove Press, 1994)

Lomax, Alan: *Folk Songs of North America* (Doubleday, 1960)

Lomax, Alan: *The Land Where the Blues Began* (Pantheon Books, 1993)

Manley, Roger: *Weird Louisiana: Your Travel Guide to Louisiana's Local Legends and Best Kept Secrets* (Sterling, 2010)

Neville, Art; Neville, Aaron; Neville, Charles; Neville, Cyril; and Ritz, David: *The Brothers — An Autobiography* (Little, Brown & Co., 2000)

Pascoe, Jill: *Louisiana's Haunted Plantations* (Irongate Press, 2004)

Rose, Al: *Storyville, New Orleans: Being an Authentic, Illustrated Account of the Notorious Red Light District* (University of Alabama Press, 1978)

Saxon, Lyle: *Gumbo Ya-Ya: A Collection of Louisiana Folk Tales* (Louisiana Library Commission, 1945)

Schafer, Judith Kelleher: *Brothels, Depravity and Abandoned Women: Illegal Sex in Antebellum New Orleans* (Louisiana State University Press, 2009)

Sillery, Barbara: *The Haunting of Louisiana* (Pelican, 2001)

Starr, S. Frederick (editor): *Inventing New Orleans: The Writings of Lafcadio Hearn* (University of Mississippi Press, 2001)

Tayman, John: *The Colony — The Harrowing True Story of the Exiles of Molokai* (Scribner, 2006)

Tidwell, Mike: *Bayou Farewell* (Vintage, 2004)

Twain, Mark: *Life on the Mississippi* (James R. Osgood, 1883)

Wardlow, Gayle Dean: *Chasin' the Devil* (Hal Leonard, 1998)

Wells, Ken: *The Good Pirates of the Forgotten Bayous: Fighting to Save a Way of Life in the Wake of Hurricane Katrina* (Yale University Press, 2008)

White, George R.: *Bo Diddley — Living Legend* (Castle Communications, 1995)

White, Neil: *In the Sanctuary of Outcasts* (William Morris, 2009)

Wilds, John; Dufour, Charles L.; and Cowan, Walter G.: *Louisiana Yesterday & Today — A Historical Guide to the State* (Louisiana State University Press, 1996)

Wiltz, Christine: *The Last Madam: A Life in the New Orleans Underworld* (Da Capo Press, 2001)

Word, Christine: *Ghosts along the Bayou: Tales of Haunted Places in Southwestern Louisiana* (Acadiana Press, 1988)